Paul Brown is a clinical psychologist, and is especially interested in making psychological knowledge and ideas widely available outside of specialist circles. After the publication of Masters' and Johnson's *Human Sexual Inadequacy*, in 1970, he was given a major research grant by the D.H.S.S. in conjunction with the National Marriage Guidance Council to investigate the development of Masters' and Johnson's ideas in a British setting, and to develop the training of Marriage Guidance Counsellors in sexual function therapy.

Educated at Kingswood School, Bath, the University of Durham and the Institute of Psychiatry in London, he is a corresponding associate of the Royal College of Psychiatrists, a Fellow of the British Psychological Society and was founding Chairman of the Association of Sexual and Marital Therapists. A frequent broadcaster, he is currently Managing Director of Frederick Chusid & Company Limited, an organization offering career counselling to executives throughout Europe.

Carolyn Faulder is an author, freelance journalist and part-time lecturer. A writer on a wide range of contemporary issues, her special interests are health and sexuality, careers information and better opportunities for women in all aspects of living. She is active in the women's movement and particularly concerned with improving media representation for women.

Formerly Assistant Editor of *Nova*, Carolyn Faulder is co-author of *The Women's Directory*, a complete self-help guide for women in Britain. She is currently running a Careers Advisory Service for *Cosmopolitan* and is co-author of the *Cosmopolitan Careers Guide*. Her other books are *Talking to Your Doctor* and *Breast Cancer: A Guide to Its Early Detection and Treatment* (to be published in 1979).

Paul Brown and Carolyn Faulder

Treat Yourself to Sex
A guide for good loving

Penguin Books

Penguin Books Ltd, Harmondsworth,
Middlesex, England
Penguin Books, 625 Madison Avenue,
New York, New York 10022, U.S.A.
Penguin Books Australia Ltd, Ringwood,
Victoria, Australia
Penguin Books Canada Ltd, 2801 John Street,
Markham, Ontario, Canada L3R 1B4
Penguin Books (N.Z.) Ltd, 182–190 Wairau Road,
Auckland 10, New Zealand

First published by J.M. Dent & Sons Ltd in association
with the National Marriage Guidance Council 1977
Published in Penguin Books 1979
Reprinted 1981

Copyright © Paul Brown and Carolyn Faulder, 1977
All rights reserved

Set, printed and bound in Great Britain by
Cox & Wyman Limited, Reading
Set in Linotype Juliana

Except in the United States of America, this book is
sold subject to the condition that it shall not, by
way of trade or otherwise, be lent, re-sold, hired out,
or otherwise circulated without the publisher's prior
consent in any form of binding or cover other than
that in which it is published and without a similar
condition including this condition being imposed on
the subsequent purchaser

Contents

Sexpieces

Introduction

We all function much better if we are fulfilled and happy in our sexual lives. If we are not, we may feel restless and lethargic, or vaguely discontented without quite understanding why. This is not to deny that some people do succeed in living celibate lives for long periods of time, by choice or through force of circumstances, without feeling either inadequate or deprived. However, this book is directed to anyone who wants to be sexually active in a relationship with a partner or with themselves.

The aim of the book is threefold. We should like to help people make bad sex good and good sex better for themselves. We should also like to offer it to the increasing number of professionals – doctors, psychologists, nurses and social workers especially – who want to inform themselves about the new ways of looking at sexual difficulties, and to loosen their professional inhibitions by developing personal ease in sexual matters. Above all, however, we should like to offer this book as a contribution to the new understanding which sees enjoyable sex as a right, not a privilege, of human beings.

The idea for the book grew from the research that Paul Brown directed for three years in the Midlands under the joint auspices of the National Marriage Guidance Council and the Department of Health and Social Security. The purpose of the research was to investigate Masters' and Johnson's methods of sex therapy with the intention of developing treatment services and making them more widely available in this country.

It became obvious as clinics were set up that, for as far ahead as could be seen, requests for help from couples wanting to change their sexual lives and relationships would far exceed the facilities that professionals in the field could develop, to the extent that waiting lists of up to a year began to build up. Paul Brown and his colleagues were committed to the belief that the best way of helping a couple was to help them learn how to be a resource to each other.

Carolyn Faulder had known of the work at Rugby since its early days and written about it for *Nova* magazine. She has also been much involved in the women's movement and self-help groups.

This book is a logical extension of the belief that couples can be a resource to each other and, given some pointing in new directions when it is necessary, do have within them the capacity to manage and control their own lives. This is not to say that it will always be easy – far from it – but the capacity to do so is there. It is written from the point of view of a man and a woman in a relationship but this is not to exclude its relevance for any couple – two men, two women – who wish to deepen their sexual relationship.

Throughout the book we describe particular ways of experiencing and developing sexual enjoyment. If these at times seem a little set-up and deliberate, then believe us, they are. Our own shorthand way of talking about these sexual exercises, which are somewhat like set pieces, is to call them 'Sexpieces'. Nobody ever danced well without first learning the basic steps and then by their mistakes as they progressed. As we shall frequently repeat, good sex is based on the skills of relating together which can most definitely be learned. This book will take you, in sequence, through a series of exercises which, if followed carefully, honestly and, most importantly, in order, will enable you to develop your own good sex.

The first seven chapters, up to Sexpiece 14, are relevant to anyone wanting to use this book practically. If you are using it to make bad sex good, then after Sexpiece 14 you will want to look at the Treatment Chart on pages 116–17 and thereafter go to the particular sexpieces for particular difficulties (18 to 25) which will lead back into Sexpieces 15 to 17 in a variety of ways. For those using the book to make good sex better, then the sexpieces straight through to number 17 will be relevant. For whatever reason you are using the book do follow it through, in sequence, at the speed of progress that is right for you.

Apart from Sexpieces 4 to 8 we have resisted describing the treatment programme in a day-by-day sequence. The arrangement of your life is part of your personal responsibility. It is vital though that you do plan your private time. Give yourselves enough time to explore each sexpiece properly. None can be experienced effectively in less than half an hour unless we actually specify a shorter time. Find time that is not tired time. Keep personal time for deliberately sharing the pleasures of your body with another person who is sharing them with you. Personal private time is a very rare commodity but you can find it for yourself if you choose.

The book is structured around typical weekly meetings with a sex therapist and the chapters should be followed on at least a week-by-week schedule – if not quicker, then certainly not slower. Should any sexpiece not work for you, try to find the real reason for this. Just saying, 'I don't like it' will not do. Examine the feelings beneath such a judgement. You may sometimes find a valid reason for not getting into a particular sexpiece; you may still be feeling uncertain or anxious. Do not expect, however, to grow easily into later sexpieces if an earlier one has not worked. You might, but we would be surprised.

One last word. All the case material in the book comes from professional experience, but none of it describes the actual detail of a specific couple. The cases are composites.

Enjoy your own discoveries!

London   Paul Brown
January 1977   Carolyn Faulder

1. Yes, another book about sex

We come into the world because of sex. The sex that we are, and the sex that we have, shape our lives. The sex that we are we cannot change, but the sex that we have, we can. This book is about making the sex that we have the best it can be.

One of the first questions a young child will ask of its mother is, 'Where do babies come from?', but long before it has come to the point of formulating this relatively sophisticated inquiry in its own mind, it will have become pleasurably aware of itself as a sexual being. The new-born baby, pummelling and kneading its mother's breast as it pulls greedily on her nipple, has learnt, almost with its first gulp of her milk, that those soft, warm, deliciously scented cushions provide pleasure as well as nourishment. It accepts both without questioning, guilt or anxiety. As the baby gets older and wiser, it will often continue sucking long after it has emptied the breast, just for the delight it offers and the chance to curl tiny, exploring fingers over the beautiful curves. Replete and content, it will fall asleep, a satisfied smile replacing the greedy activity of a few moments before. If, as a privileged onlooker, you were to look up at the mother's face, you would see the pleasure shared. She is experiencing not only the joy of being able to feed her baby from her own body but a profoundly erotic response to this union, sometimes to the point of orgasm.

This close physical contact between mother and child – mouth to breast, skin against skin, eye to eye – is the first sexual communication we make with another person. It is uncomplicated, natural and completely free from a sense that something nasty or dirty is happening. It expresses love and understanding and the need human beings have for each other, emotionally and spiritually, as well as physically. It is a perfect example of what good sex is about.

Shocked? Breast feeding a sexual activity? Do you think that this is a typical exaggeration, and only to be expected from people who have got 'sex on the brain'? Even if you do, we think you will get something from this book.

Although the subject of sex dominates our lives in so many ways – through the books we read, the films we see, the advertisements we subconsciously absorb, the conversations we overhear, the discussions we join in, the relationships we have with friends, parents, teachers, lovers, employers, workmates – for many of us, even those who could technically be described as 'sexually very experienced', sex too often remains a 'subject' of interest; a 'matter' for concern or regret or disapproval or unhappiness or repression, an 'activity' either tacked on to our everyday lives or regarded as something at which we aim to excel, but which frequently and inexplicably lets us down. Sex in its most important aspect – sex for pleasure, for fun, for fulfilment – continues to elude us. We want to enjoy it and we want to share our pleasure with our partner, but we frequently fail and we cannot understand why.

Depending on our mood, our state of health, our financial situation, our job, our day-to-day relationships with people we love, like or dislike, our own self-esteem, or lack of it, so too our enjoyment of sex, and our need for it, waxes and wanes. What should not change, however, is our inner conviction that good sex is always worth achieving. The fulfilment and delight it brings go far beyond the beginning and end of orgasm. Good sex is not just about intercourse and how to achieve maximum physical satisfaction. Good sex makes us feel good about ourselves and feel good about the way other people make us feel. It meshes into all our relationships, women and men together – whether one-to-one or in group contact – men together, women together. A good sex life overspills into all our other activities and influences the attitudes we adopt and the way we feel about everything from facing the bank manager to coping with the daily chores.

Now if that sounds like an over-rated claim for sex, a bit too much like the message on the label of one of those old-fashioned medicine bottles which promise that The Mixture will cure everything from piles to manic depression, just stop a moment and think of all the unpleasant effects a bad sex life can produce. Apart from feeling miserable and fed-up most of the time, people who are not enjoying their sex life will find that everything else that they do also loses its edge and glitter. Often, because this side of their life is so incomplete and frustrating, they will try to over-compensate in other directions, either by burying themselves in their work, drinking too much, polishing the furniture until their unhappy face glowers back in reflection, or by taking it out on everyone who crosses their path. The worst thing about their un-happiness is that most certainly they are quite unable to discuss the situation with the one person who matters most and is closest to them, their partner. It is not unknown for married couples to live together in a state of mute hostility, possibly even continuing to share the same bed for years on end without ever coming together in a loving embrace, never being able to bring themselves to do the one thing which might lead them back to each other, which is to talk about their relationship. Most people are deeply pessimistic about being able to change themselves. It is not sur-prising that in the highly sensitive area of an intimate relation-ship we are afraid of the wounds and humiliation that we might inflict and suffer, but alone of all the animals that have ever in-habited this earth, human beings have the capacity to change themselves and their lives. This book is about learning to do that.

Ideally, if you are one of a couple, you will read it together and enjoy the sexpieces together, unless it happens to be a sexpiece for one person to do alone. If you are single, whether temporarily, voluntarily or more or less permanently, there still remains much that is relevant. Celibacy does not automatically mean a deprived sex life. Masturbation, far from being a poor substitute for the 'real thing' can sometimes provide as much pleasure and satisfac-tion as sex with a partner, sometimes more. As a means of learn-ing about our own body, and what gives pleasure and how, it is essential to our full sexual self-realization. Feeling at ease with our own body is vital to feeling at ease with our lover and, therefore, vital to good sex.

These are some of the things people say to us:

'Sex just doesn't work for me.'
'Sex isn't what it used to be.'
'I can't get aroused, whatever my partner does.'
'I can't get a climax.'
'I'm not sure if I've ever had an orgasm.'
'I don't seem to enjoy sex like my friends say they do.'
'I don't seem to be as good at sex as my friends say they are.'
'I just don't get turned on any more.'
'Maybe I'm getting too old.'
'I seem to have lost interest.'
'I'm worried because I know my partner doesn't enjoy it.'
'Sex is a bore.'
'Sex is marvellous but I seem to have lost the knack.'
'Sex is marvellous. Can we make it even better?'

If you can identify with any one, or more, of these statements, then we can promise you that this book will help you. However, we can only give you the route; you will have to make the journey. You know the sort of person who writes off for countless holiday brochures about exotic places but never quite commits himself to the effort and excitement of getting anywhere. Many people are like that about sex. How often have you heard someone say that he is afraid of flying, or does not like long journeys, or cannot stand crowds at stations and seen him use these excuses for limiting his life? If this book is going to help you in your own self-discovery, then it requires from you a willingness to learn, not by getting a few rules off by heart and hoping that the results will follow as if by magic, but by *doing*.

Remember, sex is an activity, sometimes solitary and sometimes mutual, but whatever else, it is about doing things, so it is no good lying back and thinking about England. We must also get away from the idea that a man puts on a performance and a woman passively accepts. Sex is a shared pleasure which both people actively give and take.

Sex is also a skill and, like any other, the better we can learn it, the more our competence will please us. Good sex does not come naturally if by 'naturally' we mean that it is inborn. You may be one of those fortunate people for whom sex has always been spontaneously good, but that depends largely on the quality of the emotional experiences that you have had from the first day you came into the world. If, however, sex has not always been very good for you, it is never too late to learn how to improve the quality of your adult emotional and sexual relationships.

When you think about it, everything else we do is a learned skill from the time when, as small children, we learned to repeat words after our mother. Then, as we grew older, we learned to string them together in sentences. Learning to eat, learning to dress ourselves, learning to read and write, learning a job, learning to play a game, learning to do anything from the most simple to the most complex activity requires someone to teach us how to do it. Alas, sex is the unique exception. No one teaches a child what to do sexually; it is merely told, more or less adequately, about what happens, with rats or rabbits or fish as examples, hardly creatures with which the young human can identify easily. Indeed, the very idea that young people who are given sex education in school might be tempted to put into practice what they have learnt off the blackboard has led some educationalists to suggest that sex education should be restricted rather than expanded.

Does it not seem extraordinary that learning about one of the most important human activities is left entirely to chance and our friends? If you are very fortunate, your early sexual experiences will have been with someone who is older, more experienced and combines the fairly rare personal qualities of tenderness, patience and sympathy to help the fumbling beginner. Learning together about sex may seem like love's young dream, but in reality it often ends, if not in disaster, then in unfulfilled expectations.

As sex is a skill, so good sex is an art and again, like any other, it can be developed and transformed into an enriching experience. But, like any art, it needs time and dedication to unravel its mysteries and to discover the potential that lies within all of us to be great lovers, if only we want and care enough to excel in this capacity.

Above everything, time is what we must be ready to give ourselves to make sex good. Oddly enough, personal private time for sharing bodily pleasures so easily gets written out of our lives. Reflect on how much time we are prepared to devote to other activities that we enjoy, like reading a book, listening to music, watching television, doing a hobby, training for some sport, even walking the dog, and it makes us realize how anomalous this is. We can think so much about sex, talk about it so often in an abstract way, yet when it comes to doing it ourselves we tend to treat it as if it were the last and least important event in the day. We sit up late yawning in front of the television set, drag ourselves wearily to the bedroom, wash and undress hurriedly and flop exhausted into bed. How can sex be a pleasure if we are not willing to give ourselves any time to enjoy it?

We need time to discover what it is that pleases us and how to experience that pleasure. We need time to think about our pleasures, to fantasize about them and talk them over with our partner. We need time to explore our responses, to experiment with ourselves and our partner. We need time to spoil ourselves, to be unashamedly self-indulgent. Just imagine the time and careful preparation you are ready to lavish on cooking a really delicious meal for friends or the close attention you will pay to every detail of planning a holiday and then compare it with the way you made love last night, last week or last month. Perhaps you cannot even remember, so boring, automatic and rapid a routine the whole thing has become.

Later in this book we shall talk much more about the ways and means of restoring excitement and pleasure to your love-making, or indeed perhaps learning for the first time how to treat yourself to sex. Many of the sexpieces are devised to reawaken our sense of touch, so crucial but often so neglected even in our most intimate relationships. It is a sad fact that there are many families living together for years who hardly ever exchange an embrace, a hug or a kiss. Boys particularly suffer from this no-touching prohibition because it is felt in our stiff upper-lip Anglo-Saxon culture that too much open display of affection will make them soft, or turn them into homosexuals. Try and remember when you last saw a father kissing his teenage son or two men friends embracing each other. Yet men in Latin countries do not have any inhibitions about touching each other, kissing each other, even weeping openly if they feel so moved. The British, who find it painful even to shake hands, except on the most formal occasions, have something important to learn in this respect.

This brings us to our first sexpiece.

Sexpiece 1

Set aside an hour for yourself when you know that you will not be disturbed. Perhaps it is in the middle of the day when the children are at school and you have your home to yourself, or maybe, if you are both working all day, you can take it in turn on two different evenings to start preparing for bed an hour earlier while the other watches television or is out at an evening class. If you are living on your own, finding the occasion will be no problem but whatever your circumstances, do determine that you are not going to allow yourself to be distracted from yourself for any reason. Make sure that your bedroom is warm. Close the curtains and, while you are running a hot bath, undress slowly. If the telephone rings, ignore it, or take it off the hook before you start.

Stand in front of a full-length mirror – every bedroom should have one – and look at yourself all over. Try and imagine it is the first time you have seen yourself naked. Indeed it may be a very long time since you really looked at your body. Decide what you like about yourself. Familiarize yourself with the shape of your body. If you catch yourself noticing mainly the things that you do not like about your body, try deliberately to think of them not as 'special peculiarities', which is passport language, but as 'things special about me'. If a man selling a Volvo car spent all his time explaining to this prospective buyer why it was not a Rolls-Royce, he would be doing the manufacturers, his customer and himself no good because he would not have conveyed the unique and special characteristics of the car that he was offering. He would have diminished its individuality by comparing it with an inappropriate ideal of perfection. Many of us behave like this all the time about ourselves. We pay much more attention to our supposed faults and shortcomings than to our strengths and good qualities.

Accept your body as it is. Look at the way your pubic hair grows, the size and colour of your nipples. Look at the shape of your hips, the set of your shoulders, the roundness of your bottom. Explore the sight of your body. We are not going to tell you exactly what to do because learning to use your imagination is essential in learning how to make sex good. You will find that all these sexpieces demand mind involvement as well as learning how to use your body. Sex is not just in our genitals; it is in every bit of our body and in our head and our heart as well.

When you have finished looking at yourself really well, back and front, climb into your bath and now start exploring your body with your hands. Soap them first so that they run smoothly and softly over your skin. Do not use a flannel because that will numb the contact. Do it slowly and thoroughly, letting your hands go all over you, using your fingers to go into all the holes and hollows, folds and crevices, round the curves and over the sharp bits. Let them linger and circle and rub a little, pinch a little. Notice how different your skin feels in different places – hard and horny round your ankles and under your toes, very smooth inside your thighs, a bit bumpy or pimply where hair grows, thick in some places, thin in others – and everywhere you touch you have a different sensation. Do you? Or are you not letting yourself feel too much? If not, why not?

Do not let the bath get cold but when you have searched yourself thoroughly, be aware of your skin as you dry it with a towel and its silkiness as you smooth in talcum powder or body lotion. •

Now lie on your bed and ask yourself what you think about this sexpiece. Does it seem nasty to be touching yourself in this intimate, searching way? In that case, perhaps it also seems nasty when you make love with someone so you do not let them touch more of you than you can help. Or perhaps it seems a very peculiar thing to be doing to yourself? Maybe then you think making love is also rather odd, so you try not to think of the strange position you may get into or how you may look or of the noises you want to make. In that case, if you stick with this book you are going to discover that the whole of sex is crazy. Did the sexpiece bore you or surprise you or excite you? Did it seem a waste of time? Were you a bit frightened?

Whatever your reaction may have been, try and understand why you had it or, if that is a bit too much to ask you at this stage, when you are still trying to discover how you feel about sex, just compare the sensations you had when touching yourself to the sensations you have when these five different people touch you:

> a stranger
> a friend (one of each sex)
> someone you have once slept with
> the person you are now sleeping with.

Which contact comes closest to the sensations you had in the bath, or are none of them remotely similar? If you did excite yourself in the bath, what do you feel about it now? Ashamed, guilty or delighted? Feel free to feel good. Has it ever occurred to you that to feel bad about something which is given to us for pleasure might be quite contrary to our natural impulses?

Like any other skill, driving a car for instance, it can be positively harmful to continue doing things wrong in your sex life, or not as well as they might be done. Bad habits become entrenched until it becomes very difficult to stop doing them, even when their bad effects have been explained to us. To extend the car analogy a bit further, if you insist on resting your foot on the clutch between changing gears, you will in the end destroy the clutch. Similarly, if your way of making love has slipped into a careless, hasty routine, it can destroy your marriage.

Sexpiece 2

There is a lot of thinking and, we hope, talking to be done as you get into the sexpieces, but right now – and for the only time in the whole of this book – there is something that we want you to stop doing. For the time being stop making love. This does not mean, of course, that you should stop being close to your partner – sleeping together, touching each other, above all talking to each other. Just stop short of full intercourse. •

The notion that sex must always end in intercourse is one of the things which make bad sex bad and good sex not always as good as it might be. Do not worry about making mistakes. We learn from our mistakes, as long as we can talk about what went wrong and discuss it openly. In the next few weeks you will be concerned with learning how to learn from your mistakes and learning how to talk about them honestly, as well, of course, as how to talk about the good things you discover with each other.

2. What are we going to call it?

Sex is for fun and pleasure. It is for other things too, like having children and showing someone you love that they mean something very special to you. It can also be used as a way of telling someone that you understand them or sympathize with them or want to be close to them. Sometimes it seems necessary to have sex at a very physical level, to bring about a relief of tension, and at other times, although your body is engaged in sexual behaviour, that may be unimportant compared with what is going on in your head. And there are many other situations which you can probably recall from your own experience when sex seemed to be the only right thing to do. There are plenty of good reasons for having sex and there is no particular order of merit about them.

Perhaps you were brought up to believe that sex is, first and foremost, for the procreation of children, or, if you are a woman, that whereas before marriage you had to keep yourself virginal for your future husband, afterwards your duty lay in never refusing him sex, whatever you own feelings. It used to be possible to sue a spouse for 'restitution of conjugal rights', which is a very forbidding way of describing something that is supposed to be pleasurable. Once we start thinking of sex in those terms, something to be done as a 'duty' or an 'obligation' or demanded as a 'right', all ideas of enjoying it, having fun, luxuriating in it, allowing our senses to sweep us away, evaporate in a small cold cloud of disapproval.

Stilted legal jargon is one way of describing sex off-puttingly; another is by adopting the technical words, mostly derived from Latin and Greek, which doctors, and others who are professionally involved with advising and treating people with sexual concerns, must use in their work. In a clinical context, when the doctor is making a physical examination or asking questions, it is wholly appropriate to use these words, some of which we have listed at the end of this chapter. It is also important that even quite young children should know the correct names for their sexual organs, and where they are, so that later on when they find themselves in a doctor's surgery they understand what is being said to them.

However, as we all know, some of these words are long and ugly-sounding. We find them awkward to pronounce, we do not always know their meaning and they seem alien to the feelings and responses we have about sex. We feel uncomfortable using them, yet most of the other words we have picked up here and there, through talking to our friends or reading the graffiti in public lavatories, make us feel equally embarrassed because we have been told they are dirty. Possibly we have developed our own private language which we find reassuring but would not like the world at large to know about for fear of being laughed at. So we find ourselves in a real chicken and egg situation. We may want to talk about sex but we cannot because we do not know the words to use, or else it is the words we do know which make it impossible for us to talk frankly. Yet we would not be in this dilemma if we felt comfortable about sex in general, and about sex with our partner especially. Our inability to talk naturally and freely about our sexual needs stems from one of two sources: either we do not know what to think of sex because our experience of it is so different from everything we have been told about it; or it is the attitudes and views we have about sex (never mind how we learnt them) which forbid us to talk about it – when it is good, because 'we don't need to' and when it is bad, because 'talking only makes things worse', or 'I might hurt/upset/put off my partner'.

What if 'piston' were a taboo word like 'penis'? Were people to hesitate about telling a mechanic about a failing piston in their car the way they hesitate to talk to a lover or a professional adviser about a failing penis, the roads would be littered with broken cars the way the country is littered with broken relationships. Unfortunately, people keep their broken relationships locked away in the private garages of their own misery and unhappiness.

Ideas about how men and women *should* behave towards each other, what they *ought* to do for each other and what they have a *right* to expect from one another may have been absorbed at a fairly unconscious level but they strongly influence the way we talk, or cannot talk, about sex. We must break through these barriers and one of the ways we can do this is by understanding straightaway that the only rights we have are over our own body. We can make whatever demands we like on ourselves, but in a relationship we can only ask and, as other people have an absolute right over their own body, they can give or not give, as they wish. Because one person gives, the other person is not obliged to give in return, as if the first person's giving had established a debt. 'If you loved me then . . .' Good sex comes from the sharing of pleasure, not the collecting of debts.

Now unless we can talk about sex without the 'oughts' and the 'shoulds' and the 'rights' we will never establish the pleasures of freedom, so let us examine some of our attitudes and analyse how they lead us up routes of misunderstanding into areas of guilt, blame and unhappiness. Come with us and see if you can identify with some of the difficulties we describe. And after this, we want you to use the words which really say what you mean without feeling embarrassed or frightened.

He: I know just what turns you on because a man always knows what a woman wants.

She: Do men always know what all women want?

He: Of course they do. Men are more experienced than women. Boys start earlier than girls.

She: I suppose you're right. My mother always told me to keep myself for the man I married and not to make myself cheap because men don't like shop-soiled goods. My brother could come home any hour of the night but I was supposed to be a good girl and good girls don't play around. Please tell me what I would like.

He: We do it like this because this is the way everyone does it. Enjoying it?

She: (Aloud) Mmm! Lovely! (To herself) Can't say I am. Still, I mustn't say anything to spoil his fun or make him want to find someone else.

He: (Night after night aloud) That was marvellous. You really loved that, didn't you— (To himself) She's never once come. There must be something wrong with her. I'm doing everything I know to make it work.

She: (Aloud) Yes, I did. (To herself) He just never gets me started. He says he knows everything, but I wonder if he does. He ought to know more.

He: (To himself) She thinks I'm not good enough. What am I doing wrong? (Aloud) Why don't you seduce me tonight?

She: (Shocked) Seduce you? Women don't seduce men. Don't you love me any more? (To herself) What does he mean? I wouldn't know what to do to him or what to ask him to do to me. Anyway, it's not nice for a woman to make advances.

He: (To himself) Why does she always expect me to get her going? I don't know what she wants and she won't tell me what she wants. I daren't ask her. She'd think I wasn't much of a man. (Aloud) I didn't really mean that bit about wanting to be seduced. Of course I love you. It's just that I feel a bit tired. Shall we leave it for tonight?

She: (Enthusiastically) Yes, let's. Tomorrow we'll both feel more like it. (To herself) Thank goodness for that. I'm fed up with pretending he's wonderful when he's bloody awful. I don't know what *he* wants but all I know is that I'*m* not getting what I want. Anyway what do I want? Maybe there's something wrong with me.

He: (To himself) What does she want?

Both: (Some time later to each other) I've done everything I can. It's not my fault if you're frigid/you only think of yourself.

Of course, this is a speeded-up, over-simplified version of what happens in many relationships, but by the time they reach that point this couple will be miserably unhappy, hardly on speaking terms, in or outside the bedroom, and so full of resentment and anger towards each other that they may no longer want to find out what is wrong with their sexual relationship. She feels cheated by his confident assertions that he knows all there is to know about sex when he so patently does not, but does not want to admit, even to herself, that she does not know any better herself, so she either dismisses the whole thing as a lot of fuss about nothing, or does find out – on her own or with someone else – but excludes him from her discovery. He is shaken by his lack of success but determined not to admit fault. Men are supposed to know, are they not? And he knows as well as anyone. Nobody can teach him anything. They both desperately want to know, but nobody has ever told either one of them it is not his job to make it work for her. It is her job to make it work for her.

A less drastic development of this drama happens when the couple still retain their affection for one another while accepting that their sex life is something of a let-down. Neither wants to hurt the other so they play the 'let's pretend' game.

He: I want to make you happy. You'll let me know, won't you, if I'm not doing it right?

She: Of course, darling. It's just that sometimes I feel a bit tired, but you mustn't take it to heart. I still love you.

He: (Satisfied, to himself) She wouldn't say that if she didn't mean it. She just isn't very good at it.

She: (Dissatisfied, to herself) I can't tell him the truth because if I do he'll think I'm threatening his manhood. Aren't aggressive women supposed to make men impotent?

And so they settle into a boring repetitive routine, each pretending that everything is just fine and getting through it as quickly as possible, turning over and going to sleep. Talk is the last thing they want to do. What can you say when you have built up such an elaborately artificial relationship? One brutally honest word and the whole thing comes tumbling down like a house of cards.

For both these couples, and the millions like them who can tell similar tales, the basic trouble lies in the things they learnt as they grew up. They have been brought up to accept certain stereotyped views of the male and female roles in life. Men are the active, aggressive, sometimes violent leaders; women are their passive, submissive, undemanding followers. Men know and command, women listen and do as they are told. Women are allowed to give the come-ons but men have to take the lead after that. Naturally, the more thoroughly we have been conditioned to believe that our behaviour is controlled by the sexual accident of our birth, the more difficult it is going to be for us to unlearn the damaging habits that such beliefs encourage.

Let us talk out one more common misconception about sex which will show how such attitudes can ruin our sexual pleasure, before we move on to introduce some new positive ideas into our thinking about sex.

She: It's different for men. They need sex more than women do.

He: What makes you say that?

She: Well, it's true, isn't it? Remember what little boys are like – always telling rude stories and wanting to pull the girls' knickers down and play doctors and nurses.

He: Didn't you want to do that?

She: Want to do what?

He: You know, touch yourself and play those sort of games.

She: (Shocked) Of course not! I remember once how my mother got very cross with me when I was in the bath. Anyway I don't like feeling myself down there. It's dirty.

He: I suppose women are more emotional than men. They don't get turned on like we do by pictures and books and films and things. They like sex to be all lovey-dovey and wrapped up in pink ribbons.

She: That's right. A woman wants a man to be kind and gentle and not bother her too much. My mother always said that my father was very good that way. (To herself) I don't know why everyone makes such a fuss about sex. It's messy and untidy and the best thing about it is when it's over. It's disgusting, the things some people get up to in bed.

He: (To himself) If I don't do it, she'll think I don't love her any more or that I've got another woman. If I do do it, she'll lie there like a cold rice pudding and I know she'll be thinking about the shopping or Bobby's school report.

Both: (To themselves afterwards) Why did we bother?

Perhaps you recognize some aspect of yourself in these dialogues or remember experiencing a similar situation. Even if you do not identify very closely with these particular attitudes, are there other problems about sex which you feel ashamed to admit to? For instance, if you are a man do you fear that your penis is too small to satisfy your partner? If you are a woman, are you frightened of letting yourself go, literally abandoning yourself to your senses, because you think that it is not quite nice for well brought up ladies to lose control of themselves, and it certainly is not dignified? Alternatively, do you long to experiment with your sexual life and try out new things with your partner, but are you afraid of asking because (if you are a man), she will think you are a crude beast, or (if you are a woman), you will destroy his illusions about you or you will hurt his feelings by implying that what he is giving you is not right?

There are as many secret fears, guilts and evasions about sex as there are people to have them and most of them we hug closely to ourselves, because we dare not admit our ignorance. Paradoxically, in an age of apparent sexual permissiveness and enlightenment, it becomes even more difficult to admit that after all you just do not know where or how to start improving your sex life. Ignorance breeds shame. Shame breeds a sense of inadequacy which in turn creates guilt, and when we feel guilty we have to blame someone, either ourselves, in which case we become ever more unsure of ourselves – and lack of sexual self-confidence is a sure way of making sex go very bad indeed – or we blame our partner which has the dual effect of destroying their confidence and warping our sympathy. No relationship, sexual or otherwise, can survive a prolonged siege of recrimination and accusation.

Earlier we referred to the age we live in as being permissive and enlightened. Sometimes those words are too much bandied about and they can be used to excuse attitudes and actions, particularly when expressed in public life about or by public personalities, which many ordinary people find vulgar and offensive. However, in two very important respects it is absolutely true that we were the first generation to be living in an entirely new age of sexual emancipation. Two discoveries have given us our freedom.

The first is birth control which, in the course of fifty years, has progressed from being thought of as something vile and against nature to being accepted as essential for the well-being, indeed survival, of our modern society. Furthermore, in the last ten years with the advent of the pill and other methods of contraception, including vasectomy for men, birth control is coming nearer and nearer to achieving its twin aims of being totally reliable and totally safe. Although at the present time no method can claim 100 per cent efficiency and although women are right to be cautious about the side-effects which may be induced by some methods – the pill and the intra-uterine device (IUD) especially – it is not too exaggerated to say that the overall effect of acquiring this freedom to control our fertility is revolutionizing our attitudes to sex. This is particularly true for women who, at last released from the dread of unwanted pregnancies, can now start thinking about how to enjoy sex, not just endure it. People are moving away from the idea that her body belongs to *him*, to give *him* pleasure and give *him* children. As the woman assumes responsibility for contraception, so her expectations of what she wants for herself sexually will heighten and increase. At the same time she may become more acutely aware that her man does not know what she wants.

The second important discovery is the knowledge, acquired only within the last decade, of how our bodies function sexually. For the first time ever, sexual behaviour and response in normal people have been studied scientifically. You may imagine that it would be impossible to study something as intimate and private as sex in a laboratory, and that putting sex under the microscope, so to speak, is the sure way of getting no results. However, two American researchers called William Masters and Virginia Johnson overcame these difficulties and dispelled a great many myths in the process.[1] The more they learnt about sexual functioning the more clearly they realized that it is only when people are freed from fear and ignorance that they can develop a good sex life based upon open communication and a systematic discovery of the pleasures of sex.

It is evident that scientific developments and rapidly rising social expectations have combined to make a profound change in our attitudes to sex. The value we place on achieving fulfilment and pleasure from this side of our life can now be as great as we expect to receive from our work or any of our leisure activities. Unlike previous generations we now have the advantage that when something fails in a sexual relationship the world need not end in a whimper. It is not so very long ago that people who caught tuberculosis had their lives controlled and condemned by the progress of the disease. With our new knowledge about sexual function it has become possible to relieve the misery and destruction and suffering of relationships which previously we had to accept as part of the inevitability of the human condition.

Let us understand this a bit better by reviewing a few of the mistaken attitudes about sex which were revealed by the dialogues earlier in this chapter. Has it occurred to you for instance that you have a perfect right to be selfish about your sexual needs? In other words, you can be not so overweening in your demands that your partner is cowed into silence, but certain enough of yourself to guide your partner to do what pleases you if he or she has not yet understood.

The man who playfully asked his partner to seduce him was really asking her to take over for the time being the role of active initiator. He wanted to lie back, relax and enjoy her doing all the pleasurable stimulating, but he did not have the courage to admit that for once he was feeling passive and receptive in case she might think that he was being unmanly, and he was too embarrassed to suggest to her something new that he would have liked her to do to him for fear of her outraged reaction. In the same dialogue she too suffers from the same lack of self-esteem. Out of a mistaken idea that she must never reveal to him that she finds him anything less than marvellous for fear it would impair his potency, she has allowed a situation of bleak frustration and deceit to develop. Dismayed by her own lack of response due to her inability to tell him frankly what pleases her, not even sure what she likes or wants, she bitterly blames him for only thinking of himself. But what encouragement has he been given to do anything else if she refuses to ask him to please her?

Neither one of this couple has come to terms with their own sexual reality. So much of their everyday life experience has conditioned them to mask their true feelings – men do not admit weakness or lethargy or passivity, women do not stand up for themselves but always try to please others – and they bring these pretences into the bedroom. If you hold back on yourself sexually, waiting for your partner to turn you on and blaming them when they do not, then you are not being an adult sexual person taking full responsibility for your own sexuality. Unless you can learn to respond to all your feelings you will continue to stop yourself, and your partner, enjoying good sex.

The woman in the third dialogue has been so conditioned by her early upbringing to ignore sex as far as possible that the idea of seeking pleasure from it is positively repugnant to her. She does not want to think at all about what goes on below her navel, thus denying herself and her partner the chance ever to start enjoying good sex. The saddest thing about this particular relationship is that she is convinced that she is being a good wife by tolerating without objection her husband's advances, while he is resigned to accepting the social cliché that women are not really interested by sex, except for having children. In acquiring all the other habits of a shared domestic life, they have lost the only one that really matters, the habit of intimacy.

Most of us enjoy having time to ourselves, providing it does not last for too long. We think of it as precious and an opportunity to relax and be ourselves, just as we want to be. However, sharing our intimacy by being physically and emotionally close to someone else, letting them see us as we really are and seeing them as they really are, warts and farts and all may not always be so enjoyable. Eric Berne,[2] the psychiatrist who wrote so perceptively about the bridges and defences people spend so much of their time putting up and pulling down between them, said that of the many possible ways in which to pass time, passing it intimately was the most difficult.

You will remember that in the last chapter we pointed out how little time people are prepared to give to sex and, as a first sexpiece, we asked you to set aside time just for you alone to find out for yourself what your body feels like, all over. Now, if you are reading this book as a couple, we want you to set aside time at a comfortable hour for *both* of you *together*. Make sure that you have nothing urgent to do and that there is no possibility of anyone intruding on your privacy. It is quite easy to take the telephone off the hook.

Sexpiece 3

Begin by trying to forget everything you have ever been told about sex, particularly the words to use for describing it. Now look at the two columns of words we have set out below. On the left-hand side we have written down what the experts say when they want to describe either a sexual organ or a sexual activity. On the right-hand side we have written a few of the words people use when talking to each other about sex.

Experts' Words	*Our Words*
Sex Acts	
Copulation	Fucking, screwing,
Coitus	having it off,
Intercourse	making love, pulling
Masturbation	Wanking, tossing
Onanism	off, jacking off
Self-abuse	
Oral sex	Come down on,
Cunnilingus	cunt licking,
Fellatio	sucking off
Orgasm	Come
Climax	Come off
Sexual Parts of the Body	
Genitals	Privates

Experts' Words	Our Words
Vagina	Cunt, pussy, fanny
Penis	Cock, prick, dick
Testicles	Balls, bollocks
Breasts Mammary glands	Tits, boobs, knockers
Menstruation Period	Curse Monthlies
Ejaculate, Semen	Come

Now, having read straight through that list – aloud and together – each of you take a pencil and paper and make *three* columns. Write down all the words in the left-hand column in the way they are set out here. In the middle column write down the second column of words (our words). Before you start writing in the third column (your words), decide on a small prize for the one who gets the most, like a kiss or making some coffee or whatever would amuse you.

Now each of you fill in the right-hand column by yourself, writing down any, absolutely any, more words that you know for the words in the first or middle columns. When you have both completely exhausted the stock of words describing sexual behaviour and sexual parts of the body which come from your life experience, add up how many you have got and tell your partner. Then swap pieces of paper and each of you read the other person's words out loud, starting with the left-hand column, then across to the first word in the middle column and then to the first word in the right-hand column. Now collect your prize. •

What we want you to achieve by playing this word game is to break down some of the barriers you have built up over time between yourselves, perhaps by not knowing what words to use, or not wanting to shock. But why miss out on the fun? Good sex comes when we know how to express our feelings freely, by the way we use our bodies and the way we use words. The experts' words all sound very correct but they do not exactly trip off the tongue, whereas the ones in the middle column and the ones you have added are all short and easy to say, words you like to use when you are feeling warm and close and loving to someone, especially when you see that it pleases your lover to hear them coming from you.

It does not matter what words you use when you are making love so long as they say what you want them to mean and you both understand each other. We hope that by now you are beginning to break through any barriers of embarrassment and guilt. There was once a man who came for sex therapy with his wife and he blamed her for all their sexual frustration, because for twenty years she had, according to him, wilfully refused to understand that when he said, 'I'm going upstairs for a shower' what he really meant was, 'I'd like to make love to you, so come up quickly'.

If you do not explain what you mean you cannot expect your partner to have divine intuition, so it is essential that you start by shedding any inhibitions you may have about saying what you want and how you want it. Say whatever you like, in the way which sounds best to you, and take it from there.

3. Let's have the light on and look

Imagine two people standing on either side of a thick, smoked-glass partition which stretches from wall to wall and from ceiling to floor. They can see and hear each other if they talk loudly enough and mouth the words clearly but the glass blurs their outline and their speech is distorted by their efforts to make themselves heard. They can press their fingers and faces, legs and whole body against the glass, matching them one to the other so that it looks as if they are touching, yet no one knows better than the couple themselves that contact in a real sense is illusory. A man and a woman copulating obviously cannot avoid touching each other, but the contact may be brief, perfunctory and so devoid of pleasurable sensations, so utterly cold, that it may seem as if their bodies are indeed separated by a layer of icy glass.

The dialogues in the last chapter illustrated how it is perfectly possible for people to talk to each other in very intimate circumstances and yet for neither to succeed in saying what they want to say or understanding what the other is trying to say to them. The word game we asked you to play should have helped to make you feel easier with the words you choose to describe parts of the body and sexual behaviour. At the end of this chapter we shall be asking you to take this word game a stage further, but before you do that let us look a little more closely at what we are trying to describe – our bodies.

One of the ways of achieving good sex is by learning how to express our feelings freely. Communicating our feelings by using the right words is very important, but even more vital is learning our own body language. To do that we must first understand for ourselves what it is that pleases us physically and then learn to communicate that desire for pleasure to our partner. Our sexuality is part of our total self-image and the barriers to good sex are as much in our minds as in our genitals. Once we can rid ourselves of the idea that there is something either dirty or shameful about our naked bodies, especially when we are using them in an uninhibited fashion to express intimate feelings of love and desire, then at last we shall start creating a word and body language of pleasure.

Sexual pleasure is something you can create and, like all pleasures worth having, it is necessary to establish favourable conditions in which to produce and enjoy it. If you have spent much time and thought on cooking a special dinner for friends, you will also make sure that the table is laid attractively, that the room is warm and the seating arrangements comfortable so that nothing spoils their enjoyment. The pleasure you take in giving them a good evening enhances everyone's pleasure, not just in the meal but in each other's company. Good sex is created in the same way.

Try now to think of your body as a receiver of radio signals. When you did that first exercise in the bath, on your own, touching yourself all over, you will probably remember discovering parts of yourself that you had almost forgotten existed. Not literally, of course: you still had ten toes and maybe freckles on your arms but you could not remember when was the last time you had touched the skin on your inner thighs or felt that slight shiver from letting your fingers run gently over the nape of your neck. Perhaps you were surprised to discover how many different sensations you managed to arouse in yourself, simply by touching yourself in different ways. (Did you in fact touch yourself in different ways – rubbing, scratching, stroking or patting? If you did, fine. If, however, your touching was not very varied do Sexpiece 1 again some time soon. Extend your experience of touching yourself as much as possible and, whenever you bathe, concentrate on skin sensation.)

Extending the analogy, it is like having a radio set which you never tune in to more than a few familiar wavelengths. Ask yourself why you have stopped experimenting with the reception. How often have you enjoyed an unexpected programme which you came upon by chance when playing with the knobs? As a young child you may recall being scolded by an adult for 'playing' with yourself or being discovered in a secret game with a friend which seemed great fun until you were punished for being 'dirty'. Perhaps you do not think you ever asked questions or felt curious about your body, yet equally you cannot remember a time when you did not feel guilty and furtive about its functions.

Social conditioning demands of the young child that it must conform to certain modes of behaviour and control its feelings to make it an acceptable member of society. It begins by learning that to bang on the table with a spoon when it wants more food, or to throw a tantrum every time it is thwarted is anti-social and, therefore, liable to make it unpopular. We all want to be loved, so it does not take too long to apply these lessons of self-discipline to any other area of behaviour which appears unwelcome. Unrestrained emotion is also frowned upon, so we learn to hide our feelings and, once hidden, it is a quick step to persuading ourselves that they do not exist.

As our body acts as a receiver of other people's signals, and also our own when we touch ourselves or look at ourselves in a mirror, so our body transmits signals to other people which are entirely controlled by our emotions. One way or another we express what we feel rather than what we think. Too often, however, we forget, as Desmond Morris[3] put it, that 'people don't have bodies; they are bodies'. Feeling, thinking, acting and receiving are all elements of our total person, and to develop any one or more of them at the expense of the others is to cripple our healthy functioning as human beings. Yet thinking and acting are usually valued above feeling.

Let us pursue the idea of the body conceived as a receiver of radio signals. If you think of it carefully you will see that every part of it is designed to receive sensation and, for that purpose, it has five incoming channels: sight, hearing, smell, taste and touch. You have only to imagine what it would be like to be deprived of any one of them to realize how much we depend on them, both for our knowledge of the external world and to increase our own self-awareness. Indeed, we often play the game of 'which would be worse, to be blind or deaf', but it can be almost as frightening and sometimes as dangerous to lose one of the other three senses. If you cannot smell you may be spared a few bad odours and not miss too much the delicious smell of newly-baked bread or an old-fashioned rose, but you might die if you did not smell a gas leak or a fire which had started in the downstairs room. If you cannot taste you will lose the pleasure of eating good food and discerning subtle flavours; you might also eat something bad without real-izing it. And you become infinitely more deprived if you lose the sense of touch. It is no accident that the word 'feeling' is used to describe emotion as well as physical sensation, and since every-thing we experience about another person and convey to another person about ourselves is primarily based on our feelings, then the more we understand and use our feelings properly the better.

In all these examples of sensory deprivation have you noticed that we have also spoken of the loss of pleasure? This is because it is entirely through our senses that we receive pleasure. Even our most intellectual pleasures – seemingly far removed from mun-dane bodily considerations – like appreciating an abstract philo-sophical concept or the niceties of an esoteric piece of musical composition, depend ultimately on the healthy functioning of our senses.

Partial sensory deprivation makes us feel maimed and incom-plete, but the human being is marvellously adaptable and even if the pleasures derived from a particular sense are denied to us, we can usually compensate to some degree by further developing another sense. Thus blind people often have remarkable tactile powers, to the extent of being able to describe a person's features just by running their hands over the face, and deaf people learn to understand what they cannot hear by watching people's ex-pressions and reading the movement of their lips.

Total sensory deprivation is possibly the most refined of tor-tures; because it does not hurt or wound in the ordinary sense does not mean that it does not inflict damage quite as grave. Experi-ments have shown that if you put someone in a blacked-out, sound-proof chamber and encase them in cotton wool with their arms and legs spread out so that they no longer have any con-sciousness of the presence of their limbs, in other words make them feel as if they are floating in limbo, they soon start to feel frightened and hallucinate.

Pleasure comes to us through our senses. It follows, therefore, that if we are to enjoy the full range and variety of delight that is offered to us through them, we must use them. It sounds so simple yet, as we have seen, human beings are quite capable of imposing all kinds of stops on themselves for apparently rational motives but which, when analysed, may prove to be dictated by irrational fears or prejudices. Let us pick up once more the analogy of the human body as a radio receiver. Instead of twiddling the knobs perfunctorily, alighting haphazardly on a station and moving off again quickly because the transmission jars or comes across too violently, thus disturbing our muted state, we must make a conscious effort to explore gently and thoroughly the entire gamut of possible reception. So too, as we know how to turn on the radio set before we can start receiving signals, we must learn what turns us on before we can hope to derive maximum pleasure from that amazingly sensitive and delicately tuned instrument, our body.

Learning how to enjoy ourselves sexually may involve unlearning a great many prohibitions and attitudes we have absorbed or had forced upon us since we grew out of early childhood, a time when we knew nothing and learnt everything through our bodily sensations. Sexual behaviour is undoubtedly the area of human activity most bedevilled by contradictory impulses, commands and vetoes, both self-imposed and socially sanctioned. Sex can be used as a means to so many ends: for procreating, for establishing property rights, for gaining power, for asserting dominance, for making money, for appeasing demands and for winning approval, among others, that we sometimes forget that it is also a faculty for pleasure, *our* pleasure, pure and simple. It is insidiously easy to accept restrictions on our sexual behaviour which are all too successful in spoiling our sexual pleasure.

Now, in order to redress the balance and restore pleasure to its proper pride of place we are going to ask for three crucial permissions. They are: the permission to enjoy my own body – *please myself*; the permission to ask to be pleased – *please me please*; and the permission to give the pleasures which are asked for – *let me learn to please you.* In a reciprocal, loving relationship each of the partners must feel free to ask for all these freedoms and to give them. Later in this book we shall describe what they involve in practice. Just for now try asking yourself what they might mean personally to you.

Permission One – Please myself!

Say to yourself: *I have a right to the pleasures of my body. Nobody is responsible for my body but me. I am allowed to enjoy the feelings of my body. I can discover my body.*

If you are a man you may think that you have been doing just that all along. *Personal gratification has never been much of a problem. If I have wanted sex I have had it. Isn't that what's supposed to be wrong with men anyway? Women are always complaining that men are selfish about sex.*

Well, that is true, but have you ever stopped to think why? Which matters more to you – how you make love or how *often* you make love?

If you are a woman, perhaps the idea of pleasing yourself seems wrong almost, certainly not something to which a nicely brought-up woman openly admits. *Sex is for men really. I mean you can't say 'no' to a man if you want to keep him, but I can't say I've ever understood what all the fuss is about. I could live quite happily without ever having sex again. Yes, I like to keep attractive-looking. That's what I would call taking a natural pride in my appearance and women are more vain than men, but love my own body? Does that mean masturbating? You must be joking.*

We are not.

Has it ever occurred to you that the same woman who can spend so much time and money on her hair, cosmetics, clothes and figure may also be capable of totally ignoring what goes on below her navel? She may spend hours gazing at her face in the mirror and not even know what her vagina feels like, let alone what it feels like to touch it in different places.

Permission Two – Please me please!

This means not being afraid to ask your partner to please you in
whatever way you feel like, perhaps reversing roles when you
want to, the woman taking the initiative, the man waiting responsively for her to decide the action. Of course this does not
mean that one should ask the other to be pleased in ways which
the pleasing partner finds repugnant or painful or undesirable, but
in a reciprocal relationship where the three freedoms are linked
and fully accepted such a situation could not arise because the
partner asked to do something difficult or unpleasant has the freedom to express dislike.

If you are a woman, perhaps it has never occurred to you to ask
to be pleased or, equally, to indicate that something has become
boring or never was pleasurable. *If I told him after all these years
that I'd never had an orgasm, that I've been faking it because I
didn't want to upset him or spoil his enjoyment, I think it would
break up our relationship. I don't think he could take it. And
what you've never had, you don't miss.*

That is not true for a start. Being told about something good
which other people enjoy but you have never even had is enough
to make you want it very badly, and make you feel resentful
towards your partner for not giving it to you. But before you can
ask to be pleased you must know what it is that pleases you, hence
the need for freedom one.

If you are a man, perhaps there are ways of being pleased as
well as pleasing which you have never dared to ask for because
you are afraid your partner would think it showed that you are
not very manly. *If only she would start the loving occasionally.
Sometimes I don't want to do anything but be stroked and kissed
all over. I just want to lie there and have it all happen to me and
not have anything expected of me.*

Forget all that stuff about Action Man and follow your in-
stincts. You are allowed to be selfish in love, both of you. That is
freedom one and freedom two is taking turns to take advantage of
that right.

Permission Three – Let me please you!

This means finding out what pleases your partner by asking or touching or tasting, by listening and looking, and then giving those pleasures to each other.

If you are a man, perhaps you have never bothered to spend too much time asking her what she likes. *She's always seemed perfectly happy. I'd know if she was pretending and too much talk spoils sex. Anyway if she wants anything else she's only got to ask me.*

Yes, she has, but she can only do that if you both accept and offer freedoms one and two to each other.

If you are a woman, perhaps you have had a few fantasies about the things you would like him to do which you are sure would please him, but you have not dared to suggest them for fear he will think you are a tart. *Once when we had sex in a different position I know he liked it, but he's never suggested we do it like that again. I wonder why? Is it because he thinks I didn't like it or because it's too animal-like or what?*

Why were you afraid to ask him for what you wanted? Have you ever thought that by not asking him for what you wanted, you cut him off from the pleasure of learning to please you?

Let us move from abstractions to action. The sexpieces which follow are extended over five days. Each one marks a step forward. The time you spend thinking and talking about what you have done is as necessary a part of the learning process as the exercise itself. While they are addressed to couples they can almost all be done by a single person.

Sexpiece 4

Day One. Each of you takes it in turn to stand naked in front of your full-length mirror (remember, every bedroom should have one!) with your partner watching silently, also naked. Take at least ten minutes to look at yourself all over, and for this it might be helpful to use a hand mirror as well which will enable you to look at various parts of your body from directions which you would not normally be able to see.

Do this exercise in complete silence but talk about it to each other afterwards. Say what you felt about it. •

Sexpiece 5

Day Two. In the opposite order to yesterday, each of you stands in front of the full-length mirror. This time say whatever comes into your head about what you see and spend at least ten minutes, talking all the time. The watching partner keeps silent throughout. Start every sentence with 'I' and try to stick to sentences beginning 'I like', 'I feel' and so on. Try not to use sentences beginning 'I can't' or 'I don't'. If you find that it is difficult to keep up the flow, convey this to your partner, not by saying 'I can't find anything to say' or 'I don't know what to say' but express what you are actually experiencing, such as 'I'm finding it difficult to speak' or 'I feel embarrassed', or 'I feel awkward with you watching me' or whatever else you feel.

Recognize that you are responsible for your own feelings. If you convey that you feel awkward with your partner watching, he or she is under no obligation to leave or to do anything about your feelings, except to share the feeling with you. If you convey something like 'I feel good about my body' your partner can also share the pleasure of that positive feeling with you. When you are the watching partner in this sexpiece, try to listen inside yourself to your own feelings, which are the reactions of your body to the information from your partner. They will help you to understand what your partner is really feeling and really trying to communicate to you.

Discuss your body in detail and listen to yourself speaking. Do you hear yourself saying things like, 'I wish I had bigger breasts' or 'I ought to lose my beer belly'? If you do, ask yourself why you phrase it like this. Are you secretly hoping for reassurance from your partner or a flat denial that what you see is there, really is there?   •

The purpose of this exercise is to analyse the way you represent your body to yourself and if you are not representing it honestly, for instance by saying, 'I wish I could lose weight on my hips' instead of saying positively, 'I know I'm fat but I like my food too much to slim', then you must realize that you have not yet learnt to take responsibility for yourself. Until you can accept yourself, which includes your body, as you are and not for what you wish you were or regret you are, then you will not be able to think or talk honestly about yourself or your sexual relationships. A sense of self-worth can only come from within yourself and when you have that, you also have self-confidence. And please do not think that you have to be ravishingly beautiful or staggeringly handsome to feel self-confident and sexually attractive.

When you have each done this sexpiece you might like to do it again.

Sexpiece 6

Day Three. In the same order as on the first day, each of you stands naked in front of the mirror, but now it is the turn of the watching partner to make comments about the other. Again every sentence must start with, and be expressed, in positive terms. For instance, if you do not like the lumpiness of your partner's behind, say what you feel about it, straightforwardly. 'I find your behind is fat and lumpy' rather than 'I don't like ...' or 'Your behind is too ...' Both the latter statements convey judgement and criticism and your partner will feel either humiliated, hurt and stung into silence or will retaliate defensively, whereas your first statement simply tells your partner how things impinge on you.

In this way each partner will learn that what the other says is for real – both the 'good' and the 'bad' things – and it is surprisingly reassuring to have that certainty. Neither of you is obliged to give the reasons for your feelings. At this stage experience your feelings rather than struggle to understand them. •

If you did the sexpiece on day two as honestly as possible, this one will not be as difficult as it sounds, because you will have already torn aside some of the barriers to frank communication. We think you will be amazed how much more relaxed and comfortable you will feel with each other, once you have spoken in this way to each other. You may also be surprised by what you discover about each other's inner feelings.

These first three days have all been concerned with the sense experiences of sight and, to a lesser extent, hearing. These are distance senses. Now we will use hearing in a way which brings you closer to your partner and is certainly warmer.

Sexpiece 7

Day Four. Lie together in bed, or one of you sit on a sofa or in a chair and take it in turns to lay your head on the other's lap. Just stay quiet and listen to the noises of your partner's body. If you put your head against their chest you will hear their heart thumping; if you bring it down to their stomach you will probably hear it gurgling.

You may be dressed or not for this sexpiece. •

Sexpiece 8

Day Five. We are now going to introduce another sense – smell. Probably you already associate a particular aroma with your partner. We all have a natural body odour, sometimes a very distinctive one, and it may well form part of our attractiveness to our partner, without either of us being properly aware of it. By contrast animals, who are mostly rather short-sighted, are usually very keen-scented. There is, for instance, a certain type of moth where the male can smell the sexually inviting scent of the female from at least a mile and a half's distance. Any human being a fraction as pungent as that would be regarded as the reverse of sexually attractive, but we obviously appreciate the sexual power of an alluring scent, otherwise we would not spend so much money advertising and buying expensive perfumes.

Sometimes we go too far in our efforts to mask our natural smells, as in the present campaign to sell vaginal deodorants. The worst aspect of the sales promotion for this useless product is that it is directed primarily at young girls, most of whom have not yet had time to establish their sexual self-confidence. To be assaulted by advertisements advising them that the natural mild odour emanating from a healthy vagina is unclean and unpleasant – the hidden meaning behind the coy gushing euphemisms – is not only untrue but it can also be positively dangerous, if a woman, through ignorance, is persuaded that all vaginal odours can be dealt with by spraying them away. In some cases the smell will be bad, indicating the presence of an infection which requires medical treatment. But most bodily smells are rather nice, particularly when they belong to someone we love. By now you are not afraid of looking at each other's body all over, so why should you mind smelling and tasting each other as well.

For this final *Day Five* sexpiece have a bath together. Avoid putting any salts or other additives into the bath and do not powder yourself with talcum or rub in any body lotion. Go to a warm bed. Smell each other's hair, hands, behind the ears. Nuzzle each other, under your arms, behind your knees, between your toes, between your legs. Taste each other too.

Curl up together and go to sleep in each other's arms. •

4. Clearing up some worries

Before explaining the mechanical details of what is happening to your body when you are sexually aroused, we want you to begin to recognize for yourself the feelings that accompany this arousal. Any couple who are really close to each other can discover almost all the information they ever need for understanding how their bodies function from this intimacy. In this book we discuss many of the psychological reasons why men and women find it difficult to enjoy sex as much as they could or are disappointed by the reality compared to their expectations. Later on we will deal with the specific problems that individuals may encounter and describe procedures for overcoming them.

Now, however, we want to examine another cause for anxiety and, therefore, unsatisfactory sexual function which has to do with our bodies as much as our minds, but can be just as paralysing in its effects. It is also something that people find very hard to admit to, at least to each other, although internally they may be racked by fear and self-doubt. It is the dread that somehow our bodies are not quite normal, or not beautiful enough, or will not be attractive to our lover.

As adolescents experience the bodily changes that puberty brings about in them it is quite natural for them to feel disturbed. The young girl has to cope with menstruation which may not have been properly explained to her; her budding breasts, whatever their size, invariably seem to her to be wrong, either too big or too small; and if she has ever examined her sexual organs with a mirror (the majority of girls do not), she may have thought that they were ugly, even repulsive. As she is most unlikely ever to have compared them with another woman's – friend, sister or mother – she may also be seriously concerned that they are abnormal in some way. Boys at least have this advantage over girls of the same age: because their sexual organs hang outside their body and are clearly and constantly visible to themselves, and to their companions when urinating, showering and, as some do, masturbating together, they do have a good idea of what the male genitalia look like. However, these opportunities for comparison may also create considerable anxiety. Boys and men commonly worry that their penis is too small because they do not appreciate that although the size of an unaroused penis does vary considerably, when erect the difference becomes minimal. All that happens is that the large limp penis expands less when sexually aroused than the small limp one.

Another curious fact about a man's view of his body is that he usually looks down on his penis, in other words from an angle in which it appears unduly foreshortened, so even when he is comparing himself with other men, unless they range themselves in front of a full-length mirror, he still sees himself in a distorting way while he sees the others as they are. Women too, who worry about the size of their breasts, seldom stand in a row before a mirror to examine themselves as well as each other. A woman who goes to a striptease show or looks at pin-ups in a girlie magazine automatically has a mental flash of her own breasts, but she is not actually looking at them head-on when she is making the comparison so it is hardly surprising that she usually ranks herself second.

What start as normal adolescent worries tend to carry over into adult life and assume much more serious proportions, especially if there is no one to talk to or you feel too ashamed to admit your feelings. Lovers can unwittingly exacerbate the situation if, by their own somewhat furtive behaviour – making love in the dark – or never saying anything appreciative about their lover's body, they confirm the other person's suspicion that there must be something unpleasantly wrong with them. It is, after all, perfectly natural to seek affirmation, especially from those who love you, that you are desirable and special. Parents do this for their children and give them confidence to leave home and face the world as people in their own right. Unfortunately, it is a common human failing to observe and comment on the less attractive aspects of a person rather than the good.

Another anxiety many people suffer from derives from the body fluids they produce, especially when they are sexually aroused. A boy has wet dreams and tries to hide the evidence from his mother by not letting her make his bed. A girl worries about her vaginal secretions as well as menstruation, but does not dare to ask her mother or her friends about them, so she may grow up not realizing that it is normal, indeed necessary, for a healthy vagina to produce a whitish, odourless discharge, more round the middle of the month when there may also be a little spotting. (The vaginal discharge she should worry about is one that irritates or has an unpleasant smell. Never use deodorants in the vaginal area.) She may not know that the wet feeling between her legs when her boyfriend kisses her passionately is a sign that she is becoming sexually aroused and that this moisture is equivalent to a boy beginning to get an erection. Unless they are understood and talked out, these anxieties can often develop into a feeling that there is something a bit messy and disgusting about sexual excitement. But who said that sex is meant to be tidy and orderly? Clean, yes. And that brings us to another aspect of love-making which prudishness can often make people ignore.

No natural function of the body, and that includes excretion, is dirty in itself. Sneezing, sweating, shitting, pissing and menstruating are all essential ways of clearing the body of waste matter which, once exposed to the air, must be properly disposed of to avoid infection and unpleasant odours. Our noses are set in the middle of our faces so we make sure that we keep them clean, but it is horrifying how many men and women do not apply the same fastidious standards to their sex organs and back passage (anus). Sometimes this is due to carelessness, for which there is no excuse, or to an idea that what does not show does not count. If this attitude is reinforced by an underlying reluctance to touch your sexual organs, at best they will be smelly and at worst, your neglect may lead to infections. Furthermore, when it comes to being in intimate sexual contact with someone else, no more immediate turn-off can be imagined than to discover that your lover is unclean.

Here are a few simple rules for bodily hygiene which should become as automatic and regular as washing your teeth, cleaning behind your ears or taking off your make-up.

1. Keep a special flannel for washing your bottom daily. Boil the flannel regularly. If you share a bathroom do not share the flannel, in the same way as you would not dream of sharing your toothbrush or your towel.
2. When you go to the lavatory wipe your bottom carefully and thoroughly with a front to back movement. This is obviously particularly important for women who may otherwise rub small particles of excreta into the area of their vulva. After passing water it is also important for both men and women to blot away any excess moisture as damp patches of urine on your pants are uncomfortable, can cause irritation and smell very quickly.
3. Wear clean pants every day – both men and women. Do not, however, confuse the unpleasant odours generated by stale bodily fluids with the special smell we all have in our genital area and which should not be masked by vaginal deodorants or perfumes. The scent of a healthily lubricating vagina or a well-looked-after penis (see rule 4) is part of you as a person and, during intimacy, acts as a potent form of sexual attraction. These smells intensify during sexual arousal.
4. If you are a man who has not been circumcised (that is to say you have a flap of loose skin at the end of your penis), you should, at least once a day, pull back this skin (foreskin) covering the tip of your penis and wash carefully. If this is not done a whitish substance called smegma will collect, producing an unpleasant fishy smell. There is now some evidence that cancer in the neck of the womb (cervix) may be caused by poor sex hygiene on the part of the man.

A person who follows these simple rules for sexual hygiene can be confident that their sex organs will be fresh and attractively scented whenever they want to make love. Some people prefer to wash just before sexual intimacy but that is a matter of personal taste rather than necessity once you adopt the habits outlined above. After you have made love you will probably want to wipe away some of the stickiness but, to avoid turning it into a clinical cleaning-up operation at a time when you want to enjoy the special satisfaction of each other's relaxed bodies, keep a box of tissues handy by the bedside.

Understanding why we have bodily anxieties – and all of us do at some time or another in our lives – and realizing that while they are perfectly natural we must not allow them to become entrenched, should help us to overcome them. Again we cannot stress enough the importance of talking over any lingering worries you may have with your lover. Remember Sexpiece 3 when you each took turns to stand in front of the mirror and comment quite straightforwardly on the various parts of your body without allowing yourself to make any qualifications like 'I wish I was ...' or 'If only I weren't ...' Never make excuses for the way you are unless you intend to remedy the situation. Accept yourself and your lover for the unique, special couple that you are for each other. You were attracted to each other in the first place because of certain qualities. Let yourselves enjoy them.

5. I can please myself

Touch is the sense which brings us closest to another person and it is the most important in a sexual relationship.

It is interesting that we use the word 'touch' adverbially to describe mental states as well as physical ones. We talk of being 'in touch with reality' or 'out of touch with the facts' or of 'having lost touch' with either someone or some situation, all phrases conveying closeness or lack of it. This is exactly what the sensation of touch does for us in any relationship, not necessarily a sexual one; it brings us closer to someone else. In doing so, it provides us with a new dimension of information about the person or object we are touching which goes beyond words.

The moment we use the sense of touch we immediately commit ourselves to taking the relationship a stage further, whereas the senses of sight, hearing and smell tell us things about another person while we can, if we like to think of it that way, still keep ourselves at a safe distance. This explains why there are so many cultural inhibitions on touching, some of which we mentioned in the first chapter, like the taboos against growing boys showing affection physically by hugging and kissing, particularly towards members of their own sex including their father. In our society this is one of the most damaging restrictions to be imposed on people who are related by the closest human bond, and the effects, in terms of human happiness, may be grave.

The sexpieces we asked you to do on five sequential days at the end of the third chapter used four senses in a much more intimate way. We asked you to look at each other with new eyes, listen to each other with new ears and talk to each other with new words, smell each other in a new way and taste each other for perhaps the first time. You may have felt uneasy at first wondering nervously what you were letting yourself in for, even a mite afraid of appearing ridiculous and at a disadvantage before your partner, but we hope that these feelings, if you ever had them, soon gave way to a state of relaxed enjoyment. Remember the goal is pleasure, so it would be perverse indeed if anything done towards achieving that end were other than pleasurable itself. If an exercise initially seems rather strange to you, allow yourself to be stimulated rather than put off by attempting it. One of the most exciting aspects of human sexuality is the possibilities it offers for making new discoveries about ourselves and others, and enjoying the experience.

Already we hope that you are experiencing a heightened awareness of your own body and that that awareness is making you feel joyous, bouncy and quite definitely pleased with yourself. Although this may be anticipating somewhat, it is worth repeating here a true story we were told about a twenty-nine-year-old woman who had never had an orgasm until she started attending a pre-orgasmic therapy class and learnt how to masturbate. She went home to try out her new skills and was overwhelmed by experiencing not one but five amazing orgasms. She felt as if the world was exploding round her and when she picked herself up out of the glorious wreckage, she walked out of a dreary flat and the arms of a bored and boring lover, into a new job and a new home, all in the space of one week.

While not everyone would welcome or appreciate an experience with such extensive consequences, the story illustrates how good sex, in whatever form, can transform other areas of our life. The more aware we are of our sensations and the more conscious pleasure we allow ourselves to derive from them, the more in touch we will feel ourselves to be with the world around us, and the closer to reality.

Here we are at Sexpiece 9 and we have not talked about climaxes. The instruction to stop intercourse for the time being (Sexpiece 2) still holds good. What we have been doing so far is to explore the senses systematically in a non-demanding way, but now the time has come to take the first major responsibility for our own sexual function. We do it by accepting the right that each one of us has to please ourself. Touch is the most intimate sense and it is mainly touch that we will develop in the following sexpieces.

Sexpiece 9

Each of you will need time to yourself, quite privately, so plan on finding half-an-hour each, at some point in the day, when you can use your bedroom. You may have to spread this sexpiece out over two days, enabling each of you to have time alone.

Start with a warm bath, making yourself feel comfortable with your own body. Then go to a warm bed and explore touching yourself, after a while gradually letting your hands concentrate on the sexually sensitive areas of your body. For a man this is his penis, the loose scrotum holding his balls beneath it and above all the sensitive tip of his penis. For a woman this will be her breasts and the vulva, which is the area between her legs (crutch). Create an appropriately erotic atmosphere for yourself by whatever means you find helpful with the aid of lighting, music and especially the use of your imagination. Experiment with producing as much pleasure as you can by the rhythmic rubbing of your penis or around the clitoris.

Neither of you may have masturbated very often before, if at all. You will want to start feeling your genitals, slowly at first, and then increase the pressure or friction or whatever motion it is which gives you the most pleasure. Massaging yourself with a body lotion or skin oil will increase the pleasure.

If you are a man you will probably start by holding the shaft of your penis and rubbing it up and down in a rhythmic manner, slowly at first and then faster and faster as the sensation increases your appetite for more until you bring yourself to climax. As you climax, think of your partner and begin to imagine, as vividly as you can, how you would like her to produce such pleasures for you. When you have climaxed, enjoy feeling warm and relaxed.

If you are a woman, you have the advantage of both your sexually sensitive breasts and your clitoris and vagina. Let your fingers circle and probe and delve gently between the folds of skin surrounding your vagina. As you begin to feel moist and aroused, let your fingers respond to your feelings. Fondle your breasts. Treat yourself lovingly and as you begin to feel pleasure rising, concentrate on producing more and more by rubbing or stroking or whatever it is that excites you most. Follow your imagination wherever it leads you and as you become more aroused, think of your lover and what you would like from him. You may think that it is very strange to be deliberately producing pleasure in yourself because you have never before given yourself this permission. Enjoy your new freedom. If you feel good about what you are doing then you can make your own rules.

Masturbating is always something that you can do to enjoy yourself, and will be something to share with your lover. Never again need you experience sexual frustration and since we still want you to keep off intercourse, if you do feel overcome by the need for sexual relief you can produce your own climax whether your partner is with you or not. •

When you have each experienced your own pleasuring by yourself we want you to arrange the next evening for continuing to learn how to please yourself – with your partner and in a non-genital way. Perhaps we should say at this stage that if, for any reason, you have found it difficult to produce a climax by masturbation, try not to get hung up about it. Sexual capability depends on your starting point. It is difficult to dive from the top board if you have not learnt how to go in from the side, but try and stick with the good elements of the experience you have given yourself, and repeat them whenever you can.

Sexpiece 10

Undress in a warm bedroom. Make yourselves comfortable. Keep the lights on. Decide between yourselves who is going to be the active partner who then requests the inactive partner to lie in whatever position suits him or her. The active person touches the inactive one all over – hair, feet, legs, ears, everywhere except the obvious sexually sensitive zones.

If either of you becomes sexually aroused, enjoy the sensation, but let it come and go. Do not try to take it to climax.

Although only one of you is actively pleasure seeking and learning quite deliberately how to extend your enjoyment of the other person's body through all your senses, the inactive partner has an equally important role to play.

Note that we say 'inactive' which is quite different from being 'passive'. Your job is to become aware of the different sensations you experience as your partner's hands explore your body. You should remain silent unless the sensation is positively unpleasant, but if you do not like being tickled between your toes or scratched under the chin, then tell the other person what is actually happening, like, 'It tickles between my toes'. Avoid repressive statements like 'Don't do that', or 'You know I hate that'.

The reason why information should only be given when the sensation is unpleasant is because at the moment the only important objectives are for the active partner to learn how to please him or herself with the other person's body, and for the inactive person to experience the sensation inside their skin.

You will find that the more pleasure you give yourself the more pleasure your partner will be receiving, so although the sexpiece is basically a selfish one – establishing *my* pleasure to please *my*self – it is reciprocal. •

Sexpiece 11

On the next night, reverse roles. •

Enjoy yourselves, but remember, please don't have intercourse yet.

6. Let's look again

This chapter is about understanding the shape and structure of our sexual organs and discovering some of the facts about why they work the way they do. The most important point to grasp is that, despite apparently different actions and reactions experienced by men and women during sexual arousal, the underlying principles are exactly the same. It has only recently become possible to understand this because of the wealth of new information about the way a woman's body reacts during sexual arousal given to us by the research studies of Masters and Johnson.[1]

Remember what we said earlier about a couple having almost all the information they ever need readily at hand providing only that they have the good sense to use their senses, in other words by looking and touching and exploring their own and each other's bodies. The purpose of the next sexpiece is to learn about your physical appearance.

Sexpiece 12

Let the man be the learning model first. He should lie on his back on the bed or the floor with his legs bent and open and his partner kneeling between them, facing him. Of course, you will both be naked and you will have created a relaxed and tranquil atmosphere for yourselves at a time when you know you will not be disturbed. By now you should be feeling so much more at ease with one another that just seeing you (the woman), kneeling there may make him excited enough to get an erection. If this happens, get him to close his eyes and lie quietly, perhaps thinking of something totally different like an incident at work or a conversation he has had with a friend. If this still does not work, try talking to him about some problem you share – your children, a bill, a house repair – in short, anything but sex, and it is probable that his erection will disappear at once, which is itself an interesting example of the way our anxieties affect our sexual functioning. By eliminating as far as possible any visual or psychological stimulation you will see that the penis responds by softening and shrinking back to its usual limp state.

Now start to examine his sex organs, feeling free to touch every part. Lift his penis and see where the shaft is joined at the base to the crinkled dark-skinned bag (the scrotum) which contains the balls (testicles). Hold the scrotum *gently* in your hands and feel the way the balls move around inside. Note how flexible the scrotum is and, in its unaroused state, how soft it feels. It changes size and texture according to temperature; when he is cold it retracts, becoming smaller and harder in order to keep the production of sperm within the testicles at the correct temperature. Similarly, when he is aroused it feels much harder and more compact.

Laying his penis on the flat of your hand, have a look at the tip end which is in the shape of a knob. If he is circumcised, this knob will be clearly apparent and right at the tip you will see a tiny hole. Through this hole passes the urine and, when he is sexually aroused to the point of climax, this hole is also the outlet for a milky white fluid called semen which he spurts out (ejaculates). (We will explain later how it is that there is never any danger of a man urinating into a woman during sexual intercourse.) If he is not circumcised, the knob of the penis will be covered by loose skin called the foreskin (prepuce). Pull this back gently and see how the knob slips out, exposing a ridge running right round the shaft of the penis at the base of the glans. This is called the coronal ridge. If you lift the penis up and look at the underside you will see that the ridge tends to flatten at the point where the glans joins the shaft. This is called the fenulum and it, together with the whole underside of the shaft, tends to be the most pleasurably sensitive area of the penis.

Before we go on to consider the internal structure of the man's genital organs and the inter-dependent mechanisms which lead to orgasm, it is now the turn of the man to look at the woman. Incidentally, you should be talking to each other all the way through this sexpiece, the passive partner showing the other where to look and how to touch, especially if there is any danger of unintentional rough handling causing pain. However, do not forget that if either of you feels uncomfortable during this close scrutiny, it is important to say so, not being afraid to use the 'I' language we talked about earlier. Do not continue with your observations until you have talked out your feelings and tried to explain what is troubling you. •

Sexpiece 13

It is now the turn of the woman to lie back and let her partner examine her; he will be in a kneeling position between her bent and open legs. In her case it is even more important that he should be telling her what he is seeing and what each part looks like to him. Bearing in mind the comparative inaccessibility of her sexual organs, she should hold a hand mirror between her legs so that she can see for herself what he is talking about and what he is doing. As he touches her, especially as his fingers begin to probe within the folds of skin surrounding her vaginal opening and move upwards towards her clitoris, she too may feel sexually aroused. She will recognize this by the sensation of swelling (congestion) and moistness (lubrication) which can be subdued in the same way as we described for the erection, although lubrication around the vaginal opening will not suddenly disappear once it is there. It is the production of more lubrication which is prevented, just as the erection becomes limp by switching off from sexual thoughts.

Look at the triangle of hair (pubic hair) and place the flat of one hand in such a way that it covers the bottom part of the triangle with the hand lying horizontal and the fingers pointing towards her navel. Press slightly and you will feel a firm bony structure beneath the fleshy mound (mons pubis) that your palm is resting on. The area from the mons pubis and down between the legs is called the vulva and it is covered with pubic hair.

Begin by parting the fleshy outer lips (labia majora) to disclose the hairless inner lips (labia minora) which vary very much in size and may sometimes be seen protruding through the outer lips, before they are parted. The area revealed will have a pinkish-reddish coloration about it, although in places it may appear quite dark, almost black. If the woman has not become moist, it may help to have some lubricating jelly (KY jelly available from any chemist), to prevent friction.

With the outer lips well separated, observe how the inner lips form a shape like a stretched-out circle. Imagine a line from the mound of the mons pubis going between the legs to the back passage. The circle is stretched so that it narrows at the top and bottom of this line. Look at the lower end of this elongated shape and you will see the folds of the vaginal opening. A little above the vaginal opening is a hole (urethra) through which urine is passed, but it may be so small that you have difficulty seeing it. Further above this and coming up towards the underside of the mons pubis is the point where the inner lips meet in a hood and, just inside this hood, is the carefully guarded clitoris.

The clitoris varies in its appearance from woman to woman. In some it may be no more than a slight, pearly knob, no larger than a small pea. In others it may be a small organ about a quarter of an inch long. Whatever the size, however, it is a mass of nerve endings and extremely sensitive to direct touch. Some sex manuals suggest that the clitoris and penis are very much the same. In consequence, men often think that the clitoris will enjoy the same hard strong rubbing that excites the penis. Nothing could be further from the truth. In practice, think of the clitoris as being sensitive in the same way as an eyeball. No wonder that it is safely protected in its own fleshy hood and underneath the strong bone which creates the mons pubis. In Sexpiece 15 and 16 there will be an opportunity to discover how stimulating the clitoris works for your partner.

Some women have now learnt to examine the interior of their vagina in the same way that a doctor does when he makes an internal examination. They use an instrument called a speculum which is made of plastic or steel and looks rather like a duck's bill which they insert and then open gently to part the walls of the vagina, securing it on a ratchet, so that their hands are then free to use a hand mirror and a torch. This is what they see.

The soft, nerveless walls of the vagina lead back to the neck of the womb (cervix) which is a shiny rounded knob, usually pinkish in colour, but its hue varies according to the woman's health and what stage she is at in her menstrual cycle. In the middle of this knob there is a tiny slit (the os) which is the entrance to the womb (uterus). In an unaroused condition the vagina is collapsed, the walls touching each other in folds which expand, flatten and extend during intercourse to accommodate the erect penis. It is important to realize that the vagina is potential rather than actual space; in other words, women do not walk around with a vertical hole inside them. A good diagram of the vagina and its position is included in many tampon packets.

The most sensitive part of the vagina is near the entrance in what is known as the 4 o'clock and 8 o'clock positions. As you look at the vaginal opening the point at the top, that is to say nearest the clitoris, would be 12 o'clock with 6 o'clock being the point nearest the anus. Touch the vaginal opening, going clockwise and inserting your middle fingers to about the first joint. You will find that your partner experiences most sensation from light finger pressure at the points where 4 and 8 would be on the dial.

On either side of the vaginal entrance there are some strong muscles (pubococcygeal) which give elastic tone to the vagina. Their grip is important for stimulating the man's penis when it has entered the vagina and they are also connected with other muscles in the vaginal area during the growing contractions which produce the experience of climax. These muscles can get lax, especially after childbirth or if a woman is overweight, so it is essential that they be kept in trim by exercise.

If you (woman) are not sure where they are, do this simple experiment. When you go to the lavatory to pass water, try stopping and starting the flow. The muscles you use for doing that are these same pubococcygeal ones and you should contract and relax them several times a day. Try it when you are standing at the bus stop, or answering the telephone or reading a book. Nobody will notice, but you may find the sensation rather pleasurable – and regular exercise of these muscles will considerably enhance your sex life. The best way of feeling these muscles directly is to lie on your back, bend your knees and insert a moistened middle finger into your vagina. Then straighten your legs and, if you are squeezing your muscles properly, you will feel pressure round the first joint and middle section of your finger. This is a good experience for a man too.

You will find that exploring the woman's sex organs takes longer because there are more parts to describe and they are more complex in design. Not only does the vagina contain the penis in intercourse, but it is the passageway by which a baby comes into the world, demonstrating how elastic this structure can be. All the complex reproductive organs which produce eggs (ovaries), nurture the baby while it is growing (in the uterus or womb) and deliver the baby into the outside world (via the cervix or neck of the womb and vaginal canal) are contained in a very compact fashion in the lower part of the woman's pelvis.

In order to get some sense of this, look at your woman lying on her back and observe the hip bones. Draw a line with your finger connecting her hip bones and curving downwards so that it is about an inch above the pubic hairline. This outlines the front half of the pelvic cradle, containing all the internal reproductive organs. It is a remarkable feat of design engineering. •

As we explained earlier, most women are unlikely ever to have examined their own sex organs in detail, let alone another woman's, so they remain unaware of how greatly women can differ one from another, yet still be perfectly normal. The most they may have done is to look at diagrams which inevitably become somewhat stylized since their purpose is to instruct through graphic illustration and not cause confusion by suggesting variation. The shape and size of men's sex organs are also highly individual, but because the basic structure is so much simpler it is easier to identify the various parts. Clitorises especially vary in size and even position; some are placed much higher in the vulva, that is to say further away from the vaginal opening, and this means that the woman must find the best position for herself during intercourse so that she continues to receive the clitoral stimulation which suits her. The outer and inner lips of the vulva will also vary quite considerably in shape and size.

What is above all important to remember is that providing everything functions normally – and we are about to describe how both of you can ascertain this – a woman should feel only pride and delight in this proof of her individuality. Her lover too, if he is sensitive and caring, will be able to tell her about the unique formation of her vulva and its special attraction for him, just as he may have been originally attracted by her eyes, or the tilt of her nose or the timbre of her voice. In the same way, the man will appreciate hearing from his lover what his penis means to her. Enjoying each other's sexual organs is one of the pleasures of a developed sexual relationship.

These self-examinations will have been very revealing. Now lie back and read on as we are going to tell you what happens internally during the stages of sexual arousal and climax. Reading this section demands considerable concentration as you will have to use your mind's eye rather than your physical ones to follow the intricate process of transformation and interaction which takes place within your bodies following the external stimulation each of you gives to the other. You may find it easier to understand if one of you reads it aloud to the other, pausing for discussion or repetition if something is not immediately clear.

Sexual arousal and response involve two distinct stages: input of sensation followed by the involuntary and reflex reaction of muscles. Thus there are always two aspects of the experience of sexual enjoyment that we have to consider: input producing arousal and reaction producing climax.

A familiar example of this sequence of events in our bodies is when a strong puff of air strikes the sensitive surface of our eyeball. Immediately the sensation is flashed through to the brain and the brain's reaction is to send a signal to a quite separate part of the nervous system which triggers the involuntary reflex of an eyeblink. If the puff of air is not very strong, then the level of stimulation is not enough to produce the eyeblink.

Later on we will be talking about the disorders which occur when the arousal process does not work properly, or when the reaction process fails. For the moment, however, we are going to track through what happens when the sequence of events is unimpaired.

The man

Let us start with the man. Think of the penis as a soft sponge through which blood flows quietly when it is hanging down in its limp everyday position, functioning only as a means for passing water. This soft sponge is a mass of blood vessels surrounded by stretchy skin enveloping a central tube called the urethra which conducts both the urine and the semen down the shaft of the penis and out through the hole at the end of the penis. Immediately a man receives stimulating input – either physically or psychologically or both – his body responds by pumping blood into the penis to expand the blood vessels. His penis enlarges and stiffens into an erection which, at its peak, may be jutting upwards from his body, ideally positioned and shaped, in fact, to fit into the woman's vagina which slopes backwards inside her body at a corresponding angle. A man cannot achieve the thrusting rhythm of intercourse unless he has an erection. A limp penis can, however, be stuffed into the vagina and this is sometimes a favourable way of stimulating an erection. It is perfectly natural that during any love play he should experience his erection hardening and softening as it responds to varying levels of stimulation.

Sexual stimulation produces increased activity in the heart, which begins to pump harder. As the blood is pumped into the penis it is prevented from flowing out again by what can best be described as a non-return valve device. It is part of the mechanism of sexual arousal for this to close as a means of retaining the blood which flows into the penis. It only opens quickly as a response to climax, when the blood flows rapidly back into the body and the penis becomes limp once more. If arousal is not followed by climax the valve opens much more slowly. Long periods of arousal without climax, which often happen in early sexual experiences, can produce a dull pain in the whole genital area because of the unrelieved pressure in the blood vessels. Quite a number of other bodily changes take place during a man's sexual arousal but, from an operating point of view, they do not have the same practical significance as the processes of erection; but they are all changes which are triggered by increasing blood flow. If you want to know more about them, then the book by Brecher and Brecher that we refer to in reference[1] will be very helpful.

Climax (orgastic reaction or orgasm) is a trigger response which impels the seminal fluid containing sperms along the urethra and out of the opening at the tip of the penis. A man experiences this as ejaculation and when he is able to control his ejaculatory process properly he can make his erection fully available for his partner's pleasure. We have not thought it necessary to describe in detail the reproductive male process by which sperms are manufactured, collected together with seminal fluid and then stored until needed for delivery at the point of ejaculation in its purely sexual function.

As sexual excitement mounts, the sperms contained in the seminal fluid are collected in the urethral tube before it enters the base of the penis. This tube is surrounded by strong muscles which can be felt between the underside of the scrotum and the anus. As the semen begins to collect in this part of the urethral tube, the man begins to experience *ejaculatory demand*, that is to say, a feeling that if the stimulation he is receiving at that point in time continues and increases in intensity, he will move into a further stage of *ejaculatory inevitability*, which is when he comes.

The actual process of coming is occasioned by the muscles around the urethra just behind the base of the penis at the bottom of the man's pelvis contracting rhythmically and strongly. These contractions squeeze the tube and force the semen out along the length of the penis and through the tip opening. As a slightly painful analogy, imagine a length of hosepipe lying on the ground, full of water and closed at one end. This is like the ur-

ethral tube at the point of ejaculatory demand. Now imagine
stamping hard on the hosepipe. The liquid inside will be squirted
out of the open end. Depending upon the force of the stamping,
the squirting will be more or less strong, and successive stamps
will produce more of a dribble than a squirt. The stamping is like
the spasm contractions of the muscles between the scrotum and
the back passage which surround the backward extension of the
urethral tube. It is these muscles which, when triggered by
sufficiently strong stimulation, create the experience of climax in
a man.

Just before a climax, many men experience a droplet of colour-
less fluid oozing out of the urethral opening. This comes from a
little gland attached to the urethral tube inside the body called
Cowper's gland. Its function appears to be to lubricate the tube
ready for the passage of the sperms and it may also be that this
lubricating fluid provides some nutrient for the sperms to help
them in their struggle to reach an egg by their long swim through
the woman's uterus and into her fallopian tubes. Sperms themselves are like minute tadpoles. A teaspoonful of seminal fluid
may contain many millions, of which only one will actually ferti-
lize an egg. This process can be likened to imagining the whole
population of London standing at one end of Lake Windermere
ready, on a word of command, to plunge in and swim to the other
end, the first one reaching there being like the sperm which meets
the egg. It is a pretty crowded business with wholesale slaughter
on the way.

Many people wonder why men do not pass water during sexual
arousal, since the same tube delivers both semen and urine. The
answer lies in the fact that, although the semen store (seminal
vesicles) and water store (bladder) both feed into the same urethral
tube, there are two small muscular gates (sphincters), like the
tight muscle at the entrance to the anus but smaller, which close
and open appropriately. Under conditions of bladder pressure,
when a man wishes to pass water but it is in the middle of his
sexual arousal, the gate just inside the bladder (internal sphincter)
closes automatically and the other, just outside the bladder (external sphincter), opens. The external sphincter can be brought

under voluntary control as a way of managing ejaculation, in much the same way as the small boy learns to manage his flow of urine during toilet training.

The woman

The same two-stage process operates for a woman: excitement builds up by stimulation, creating increased blood flow and eventually the muscular reaction of orgasm is triggered. In the woman, as in the man, disorders arise from failures in the arousal process or in the reaction process.

As a woman becomes sexually excited, blood flows into the tissues surrounding the vagina. Almost immediately the walls of the vagina respond with a film of moisture spreading all over them. At the same time the lips swell and part and change in colour. This lubrication-swelling phase is the exact equivalent of the man's erection and both are essential components of each person's arousal.

More is going on inside a woman's body. To start with, her vagina, which as we said earlier is a mass of folded skin in an unaroused state, begins to balloon out and elongate in a form of internal erection ready to receive the enlarged penis. As it is elastic, it will envelop and grip a penis of any size, which explains in part why the individual size of a fully erect penis does not affect the enjoyment of intercourse. The vagina is exquisitely adapted to fit and embrace the entering penis like a well-fitting glove enclosing a finger. Even further within her body the uterus is changing its position to help in the development of a climax and preparing to receive the sperm.

Other important changes are taking place in the breasts. In many women the nipples at an early stage of arousal become erect and, as arousal continues, the dark area (areola) around the nipple swells. It may swell so much that the nipple erection appears to go. As blood flow increases in the whole of the breast tissue, the shape of the breast itself may change considerably. Mottling of the skin (skin flush) may also occur during the later stages of arousal, especially around the neck and chest.

As arousal increases, the swelling of the lips around the vagina becomes more pronounced and the area around the clitoris more sensitive. The hood of the clitoris swells considerably and, at the peak of arousal, the clitoris retracts underneath the clitoral hood. During intercourse the man's penis can directly stimulate the clitoris by pulling on the inner lips, which form in the clitoral hood, as he thrusts within the vagina; or the clitoris can be directly stimulated by the woman pressing her pubic area against her partner. However, each couple must discover for themselves which is the best way for them to continue effective clitoral stimulation to maintain the woman's state of arousal and later on we shall describe some other methods. Fingers are very useful.

The final change during arousal is that the lower part of the vaginal barrel (about the third nearest the entrance) swells and thickens. This swelling has the effect of gripping the man's penis tightly just before climax and it is in this area that a woman may feel a different orgasmic response from that which she experiences through direct stimulation of her clitoris.

Generally speaking, the orgasmic response in women is more diffuse and complex than in men. The quality and quantity of orgasms can vary according to mood, partner, the way in which a woman is stimulated and the time it takes for her to come to orgasm. Sometimes it will seem to her that her orgasm is concentrated in the intense pleasure which comes to her from stimulating the clitoris; at other times she is more aware of her internal vaginal reactions; for instance the pressure of the man's glans beating against the cervix and the longing a woman can feel to be penetrated as deeply as possible overwhelms the previous sensations she may have felt from the clitoris.

Whatever the actual experience of orgasm for a woman, the bodily process is this. After the right kind and quantity of stimulation (just as for a man) a trigger reaction makes muscles around the uterus contract spasmodically, at intervals of just less than a second, which is the same rate as in men. These contractions flow through the uterus along the walls of the vagina and are usually experienced in the orgasmic platform – the swelling of the lower third of the vagina which we described as occurring towards the end of the arousal phase.

Although the basic physiological processes of sexual response are the same in men and women, in that arousal in both sexes is characterized by vasco-congestive swelling (blood filling the tissues) and orgasm is expressed in reflex muscular contractions, there are also some quite important differences.

To begin with arousal. In a man, arousal is marked by his erection but because his internal mechanism is highly specific and interdependent, any interference with any stage of the process may make him unable to achieve an erection and this is called impotence. Although a woman does not get an erection in precisely the same way, her equivalent response is marked not only by her vaginal swelling and lubrication but her clitoris will also enlarge and change position if it is stimulated. Whereas some women can exhibit all the physical signs of arousal without psychologically feeling at all excited, the reverse is true for some men who can feel mentally aroused but physically unresponsive.

In orgasm a man is incapable of more than one orgasm at a time and he usually needs some time before he again becomes responsive to stimulation whereas a woman who has once been aroused to orgasmic pitch is capable of several more orgasms for as long as she is stimulated and before she becomes physically exhausted. Another difference between male and female orgasm is that a man ejaculates whereas a woman does not.

In subsequent chapters we shall be looking at the problems which arise when any part of the sexual response mechanism is not functioning properly, and discussing ways of overcoming them. It will then become obvious that the right psychological conditioning and preparation is often as important as physical good health for satisfactory sexual function, but it should already be clear that men and women vary greatly, both between each other and within their own sex, in their readiness to respond to sexual stimulation. Men, particularly young ones, may respond to the slightest physical stimulus with an erection, whereas many women may take longer to learn about their potential for arousal and response. This is almost certainly due to the effects of cultural conditioning. Women are still inhibited from discovering their sexuality in their teenage years and one measure of this is that comparatively few girls know much about masturbation and do not have a slang word to describe it. The reverse is true of boys. We think this disadvantages the sexual development of women.

The degree and type of stimulation required for sexual pleasure does differ among individuals and it is as dangerous to generalize in this area of human behaviour as it is for anything else. Indeed the reverse situation often obtains as people get older. Men may find themselves becoming more affected by external pressures; too much work, too many mental stresses and anxieties, a fear that they may not be able to perform or 'come up to standard' combined with a natural waning of their physical powers may induce tensions which directly affect their sexual functioning. Women, on the other hand, who have experienced good sex for a number of years with one or more partners – the number is not important but the quality and quantity of the actual sexual encounters is – should find themselves becoming more easily aroused and more discerning in their sexual demands but less affected by what is happening about them.

A well-attuned couple will be able to cope with these changes in their sexual relationship by adjusting their roles to fit their different needs. For instance, it may be necessary for the woman to take the initiative more frequently and for the man to accept her help without feeling put down. Where sex has never been as good as it might be between a couple, this type of change can seem threatening and difficult to cope with. But you have already learnt much that should help you in this respect if you have read so far and done the sexpieces.

7. Please me please!

We want you to extend your knowledge of sex as a selfish and a shared pleasure by learning in this chapter how to use the other person to enhance and vitalize your own sexual enjoyment. Have you always thought that love should be selfless, undemanding and totally giving? We make no apology for standing all these 'noble' concepts upside down by suggesting instead that the first person to think of is yourself and your own selfish pleasure. It would be astonishing if that is all we were to suggest to you, but this book is primarily addressed to couples, two people in one relationship, and everything that is said to one applies equally to the other. We are suggesting that *both* of you do the taking and the giving, the asking and the responding, the loving and being loved, sometimes together, sometimes sequentially, but never that one should do something at the expense of the other. Now do you see why we want you to think of your love-making as a mutually selfish activity?

The special quality of the relationship that we hope is developing between you is that both of you are equally involved. *I give myself pleasure. I use you to give me pleasure. I make myself available to you for you to use me for your pleasure.* When both of you can say that frankly to each other, then you are in an honest and open relationship which enables you to feel free to ask for pleasure and to ask how to give pleasure; you can enjoy being pleasured and you can enjoy pleasuring. It is no longer a sterile exploitative situation where one of you is making demands or using the other's body as little more than a means of sexual release, a convenient sex object.

When that sort of 'using' slips into a relationship, all kinds of tensions and resentments begin to build up which, unless they are understood and eliminated, make for very bad sex indeed. Unfortunately, so many of our ideas about the nature of male and female sexuality are geared to making exactly these assumptions. Men, it is said, need sex much more than women. They are randy, compulsive and essentially polygamous. A promiscuous man is thought to be 'a bit of a lad', 'a great womanizer'; his virility is admired and envied and he is encouraged to boast of his conquests in bed as he might talk of winning battles in the boardroom or on the shopfloor. The same man can be a renowned rake and, providing that he has a modicum of discretion, still be a respected member of society. A promiscuous woman, on the other hand, is described as a tart, a nymphomaniac, as 'being no better than she should be' and as 'having no morals'. She will be the butt of derogatory criticism from her own sex and despised as an 'easy lay' by men. The same woman cannot be known to have a lover and expect to retain respect as a wife and mother or be welcomed on the committee of her local Mothers' Union.

Quite apart from the injustice of operating this double standard, it bears little relation to the real facts about human sexuality. Physically a man is at the peak of his sexual capacity when he is in his late teens and thereafter his potency tends to decline, imperceptibly on the whole, but quite definitely, whereas a woman's sexual potential increases and improves with age, up to about the middle thirties. Events like pregnancy and menopause, contrary to popular belief, often actually heighten her orgasmic functioning. If human beings were to act the way their bodies wanted them to rather than the way their minds tell them they ought to, we would see some very different patterns of social behaviour. For a start, it would be considered quite normal that virile young men should seek to have relationships with older women; the naïve vitality of the one would match up to the experience and the demands of the other. This combination would then be considered no more extraordinary than the other way round – young girls linked to older men – which today is regarded as acceptable and, in the case of men at least, often highly desirable and a proof of their sexual prowess. Whether it is so satisfactory for the young woman grown into middle age, who then finds herself restrained by an old man with failing powers just as she is reaching her peak sexually, is another matter.

Another bad result of 'using' people is that if they are objectified sufficiently they begin to behave in a dehumanized way themselves. Men have been persistently determined to regard women as chattels, objects, possessions, mysteries, angels – anything but human beings. Certain Early Fathers of the Christian Church even taught that women were without souls and unclean vessels. The fact that they glorified one woman to the position of Mother of God was possible only by depriving her of her essential womanhood. She was allowed to keep her womb and bear a child but the idea that it should have been conceived in the normal way by the pleasure of a penis in a vagina and that there should have been erotic delights in the making of it was apparently too impossible to consider. The reverse side of the Madonna medal is the whore image which is also as old as recorded history. Today's pin-up – all gleaming skin, plastic tits and softly brushed pubic hair – is in the same tradition; the unapproachable whore achieving perfection no ordinary woman aspires to, moulded in poses of sublime abandonment.

Many women are now rejecting this crude objectification of their sexuality – some with anger, some with laughter, some with despair – but the most positive reaction is coming from the growing numbers of women who are researching among their own sex and writing about their female sexuality as they know it to be from their own experience. Women talking openly about their sexual fantasies, their sexual lives and their sexual expectations are reversing many of the preconceived ideas about female sexuality which women themselves have so long accepted. Therapists following Masters and Johnson are developing their views too, in the light of new insights coming from the women's movement.[4]

If you need further convincing, consider the attitude of the woman who finds it necessary to use her sexuality as a bargaining counter. She deliberately flirts, teases, flutters and cajoles her way through life, offering her femininity as the final prize. Sex for her is a trading relationship; she gives only in return for what she gets and it is not sex that interests her, but cash, and the material goods that it buys. She is a teaser not a treater but sadly she is only reacting directly to the way her sexuality has always been presented to her, ever since her mother warned her about shop-soiled goods; it is a valuable commodity which she would be a fool to surrender lightly.

Just how stuck this kind of relationship can become is illustrated by the following true story. A man fell in love with a beautiful young prostitute he had been visiting for some time. She was the only woman with whom he had ever achieved erection and climax so finally it seemed only sensible to marry her. Although he now had her to himself whenever he wanted her, he still could not achieve orgasm unless he paid her, so each time they had sex together he slipped £100 in notes under her pillow. He came and she took and they both had to be satisfied by the substitution of a straightforward commercial relationship as the nearest approach they could make to spontaneous loving.

Anger is another destructive emotion in sexual relationships. If fear and insecurity make men seek to turn women into sex objects, women who discover how they have been cheated into accepting a dummy's role often retaliate by venting their justified fury and hate on the man with whom they are currently associated. One of the accusations frequently levelled against the women's movement is that women, in seeking their own sexual liberation, are making men impotent and, continues the argument, if the choice lies between a man's fulfilment or a woman's there is but one answer, the man must always come first. His masculinity must not be threatened. Even now, when it is almost generally recognized that women have a right to enjoy sex, this privilege still tends to be conceded only on the understanding that they enjoy it with, and for, a man. The idea of mutually selfish pleasure which is one of the underlying themes of this book is not accepted.

Case History 1: Alec and Joan

Alec and Joan had been married for five years and at the time they came for help both were in their late twenties with one child aged three. Their problem was that Alec was finding it difficult to have an erection, Joan had not had an orgasm in two years and they were making love less and less often.

This situation had developed since Alec, a solicitor, had moved his family three years ago from London to a country town practice. The move meant Joan losing a circle of friends with whom she had kept close contact since leaving school and becoming a librarian. She had been the first in her group to give up work for a child which had not been planned but both wanted. Before the baby's arrival Joan had spent a good deal of her spare-time energies in voluntary social work. Alec had always had an interest in local politics which he now began to pursue with more interest and time commitment. Joan, however, felt isolated in their new setting, cut off from friends, her previous job, her leisure interests and now tied down by a young child.

Alec had been the only child of parents who expected him to achieve well and praised him for doing so. There was, however, very little discussion of feelings or any difficulties he might experience. As an adult he continued to expect to be loved for doing well. Joan was the elder sister to a brother who had done much less well than her but whose efforts were always unduly praised in contrast to hers. For years she had felt thoroughly put-down.

In their new situation, Joan began to feel that Alec was neglecting her and he was in turn disappointed at her lack of regard for his job and expanding political activity. The more she criticized, the busier he became. Joan joined a women's consciousness-raising group and found support for her anger and sense of grievance. Alec was blamed for her unhappiness.

The treatment that they received involved most of the sexpieces that have already been explained and, in addition, they worked together on their specific problems of his failing potency and her lack of orgasm. (See Chapter 10, *He Can't Keep an Erection* and Chapter 12, *She Never Comes*.)

Basically they had a good relationship and once they started talking out their difficulties instead of confiding only in others, as Joan had done, or retreating into silence and work, as Alec had done, they rediscovered their sexual pleasure in each other. The trouble had primarily arisen because Joan had not realized that you can be free and still give; and be free and yet able to say 'no' without the refusal either being a put-down or hurtful.

Learning how to ask for what we want and feeling free so to do is possibly the most difficult thing to achieve in an intimate relationship. There are three main reasons why this should be so. Not all of them apply in equal measure to both men and women but see if you can recognize yourself in any of these situations.

From early childhood you have been taught not to be greedy, not to grab and snatch for things which attract you; you have been taught constraint and self-control and to 'wait until you're asked'. Of course, you by no means always adhere to these rules, but you know you should as far as possible because you are a civilized person trying your best to retain civilized standards in an increasingly stressed and stampeding world. Sex, however, is not a civilized activity in the sense that we are using the word here; there is nothing polite or withholding or 'after you please' about your natural sexual urges. On the contrary, you feel lustful and demanding and overwhelmed by a compelling desire to please yourself, no matter what, but they are the feelings you have trained yourself to control if the circumstances are not propitious to give vent to them. The danger is that you become so successful at restraining your 'selfish' desires that when you find yourself in a loving intimate situation with someone to whom you really long to give everything and ask everything from, you find it is no longer possible to act spontaneously. You may just be able to give, if you are asked, but you find it goes entirely against the grain to ask for your own gratification. In part at least this is due to the cultural indoctrination we have described, to which women are more subject than men.

In the second place there is a lurking fear that by asking we make ourselves dangerously vulnerable. We expose our needs, reveal our dependence and, therefore, it is assumed, our weaknesses. This is particularly true for men who have been brought up from an early age to believe that it is essential to their masculinity not to ask for help or admit need of any kind.

Then finally there is the fear we are all prone to that by asking someone we love for something they have not given us we are suggesting some inadequacy or failure on their part. *If you love me you would know what I want. You ought to be able to anticipate what I want before I ask for it.* We should like to take a loving pride in feeling that our lover understands and appreciates our needs as no one else can. *What will my lover think if I reveal that I have been missing out on something because he or she has not given it to me? More worryingly, what will I think about my failing lover now?*

Even if the trust between two people is strong enough to avoid inflicting implied criticisms of this sort, we may still find it very difficult to ask because, although we know full well within ourselves that something is lacking, we may not know ourselves and our body's needs sufficiently to know what it is. So we shift the responsibility and the blame on to our partner. It is possible to feel unhappy, discontented and frustrated in our love-making and yet have no idea why we feel like this.

One or all of these inhibitions may be affecting your ability to ask your lover to please you. However, in the special situation of reading this book you can begin to learn how to ask because you can be more certain that your lover is willing to give, and that both of you are learning now what and how to give.

Try this small sexpiece.

Sexpiece 14

Both go into your bedroom, undress and read this through together.

Now, kneel in front of one another wherever it is most comfortable for you both – on the bed, on the carpet, in front of the fire – wherever you are most private and undistracted. Look at each other steadily, most of all keeping eye to eye contact, allowing your gaze to wander a little initially if that helps, but not for long. Come back to holding each other's eyes. Then, whoever feels ready first, say something aloud along these lines: 'I want to give you everything you ask for, but if I find what you ask of me is worrying or upsetting, then I am free to tell you.' This is only a suggested formula and, obviously, you must use whatever words come most easily to you. Start your sentences with 'I' and do not qualify your statements by phrases like 'I think' or 'it would be nice' or 'Do you think that ...?' Come out frankly even if hesitantly with whatever it is that you really feel.

When one of you has made this commitment, then it is the turn of the other. Try not to worry if you do not feel ready yet to make it, but nevertheless convey your feelings to your lover with simple words like, 'I feel closed up still'. That gives your lover real information about you and something to which to respond. •

All these sexpieces build on each other. If you get stuck anywhere, go back to where you feel comfortable and take them in order again. If you get so stuck that it is making you miserable and unhappy, you may want to ask for help from your GP or a Marriage Guidance Counsellor or a sex therapist. Following this self-help course in sex therapy faithfully should get you all the way, but a few couples may find that they meet problems in their relationship which are too difficult for them to handle unaided. This is not a defeat but a realistic recognition of the facts, so do not feel ashamed of seeking expert advice. (For some useful addresses see page 178.)

Now we want you to move into a more extended experience of your taking responsibility for yourself, using your lover as a resource. We want you to use your own language for loving to express what you really want, and really feel, not what you think your lover wants to hear or what it is 'proper' for you to say. You are learning to take responsibility for your own thoughts and desires by expressing them in the words which suit you best. You are learning, too, how to enjoy touching – your body and your lover's body – and with that lesson you are also learning to take responsibility for your right to enjoy yourself with another person's body, providing always that that other person has agreed to be with you for the pleasure of pleasuring and being pleasured.

Before you start Sexpiece 15 we want you to bear in mind certain very important things. Remember to use 'I' language (and incidentally Eye language) in *everything* you say in your intimate relationship. Make a conscious effort to start sentences with phrases such as, 'I feel . . .', 'I should like . . .', 'I am enjoying . . .', or 'I am worried . . .' Avoid negative phrases such as 'I don't like . . .' because that tells the other person nothing about you at all, except that you are closing off from them. If there really is something which you do not like, then convey the emotion which underlies that dislike by describing it exactly as it feels to you. It can be very hard to express emotions like anger or fear or disappointment because you have trained yourself to repress them as being hostile or, in the case of an intimate relationship, as being incompatible with expressing love. The contrary is true. It is precisely with those people whom we love the most and whose company we most enjoy that we should be able to express ourselves most freely, as long as we give them the same right to express their emotions towards us, whether we experience them as pleasant or unpleasant.

Although this may be the reverse of all that you have been brought up to believe is the correct way of behaving, now is the time to reconsider your attitudes. You want to make your relationship positive, honest and trusting. That means never holding back from stating any of your feelings because you fear hurting your lover. Of course, there are right and wrong times to convey important feelings, but sensitive, practised lovers can pick up each other's complicated non-verbal signals from across a crowded room.

Guessing how someone else feels or anticipating how they will react to certain statements from you, without asking them, not only runs the risk of being quite wrong which then puts you in the position of working with inaccurate and, therefore, misleading information, but it is also deeply unfair to that other person to whom you have then denied the right of openly expressing their feelings. How often have you heard yourself saying, 'So-and-so doesn't understand me' or had it said to you by an aggrieved partner in a relationship? Until you are certain that you have given your lover the same chance for skilful self-expression that you have both learnt, then you really have no right to make any judgements, certainly not to feel hurt.

Being able to hear what another person is saying without allowing their meaning to become distorted by your own prejudices and expectations is a rare capacity but it can be developed if you are prepared to make a conscious and sustained effort to listen, and check out your understanding with the other person. Listening does not mean that you deny the validity of your own feelings. The special characteristic of evolving a mature relationship is that you learn to take responsibility for your own feelings and this means coming straight out with what you feel. You will do this by learning to express yourself in 'I' language; learning to believe in your feelings as valid; learning to listen to the other person's expression of their feelings; and learning to convey to them that you recognize the equal validity of their feelings. Plainly, there are ways and ways of expressing yourself frankly and nobody wants to hurt the person they love by unnecessarily brutal frankness, but if, in the course of expressing your emotions honestly you do hurt your lover, then that is important information and it may be their problem. You will know that you are moving into a better, more trusting relationship when your lover feels ready to share with you the hurt your words have caused. Only when you share the hurts can you share the joys.

Sexpiece 15

Decide between you who is going to be the first one to ask. The asking person then lies down on the bed, thinking quietly how they would like their lover to be near them, perhaps lying stretched out beside them, or kneeling between their legs. When you have decided, ask your lover to do exactly what you want. When you are asking you can keep your eyes open or closed, however you feel most at ease. Now start thinking what it felt like inside your skin when you were being touched by your lover in Sexpieces 10 or 11 or by yourself in Sexpiece 9.

Give yourselves at least half an hour each. Concentrate just on yourself and think only about the things you want your lover to do to you. Ask your lover in words and through touch, taking their hand to show them where to touch you and how to touch you, whether strongly or lightly, whether rubbing rhythmically or stroking – whatever you want and wherever you want. Feel free to ask your lover to roam *all* over your body. Ask to be massaged with skin lotion if that appeals to you. As you relax and enjoy everything your lover does, say exactly how it is pleasing you.

Both of you will be learning fast. You, the asking person, will at last be asking for what you really want and no longer pretending that what you are getting is right. Your lover will be gaining confidence and pleasure in learning how to pleasure you the way you want it. Together you will both be learning the pleasure of effective asking and giving.

When you have been touched and pleased all over at your request, it is the turn of your lover to do the asking and your turn to do the giving. •

Any questions?

He: What happens if I get an erection or my lover gets so aroused that she asks me to come inside her?

She: Yes. Isn't that specially difficult for a man? I mean if he has a hard-on surely he must have a climax?

Answer: That's one of those myths we've got to forget. Of course he can have a climax but it doesn't have to be inside you. We want you to learn to be able to feel excitement and climax when you are together without also feeling obliged to have intercourse every time.

She: But what happens if he comes unexpectedly? Have we got to stop?

Answer: So who said it was all over because he comes? The satisfaction of both of you is equally important. There's not much fun in masturbating him to climax if that means it's all over for you. If he does come spontaneously under these conditions, then maybe he ought to be thinking about how he's going to get it under control. (See Chapter 13, *He Comes Too Soon*.)

Did you know that while it is true that anatomically a penis belongs to the man, his erection belongs to a woman? It is because of her and his feelings about her that his erection comes and a woman needs a good, strong and reliable erection as one way of enjoying herself. If she learns how to use it to enjoy herself, she will be giving her man as well as herself a lot of pleasure, and he will feel like a man because he is giving her as well as himself a lot of pleasure. Later on you can teach yourself how to make it safe and strong and reliable. Just for now stop worrying and start enjoying yourself. See what happens when you say, 'Please me please!'

He: Are you talking to men or women?

Answer: Both.

8. Let me learn to please you

Sex, as we have already said, is an art and, like any other, requires a maximum amount of application, thought and imaginative skill; even dedication is not an inappropriate word when so much intense pleasure can be your reward. Unfortunately, we still suffer from many puritanical hang-ups about sexual pleasure; we think there must be something wrong with us – 'sinful' those of us who have had a religious upbringing may call it – if we admit to revelling in the sensations our body gives us; and we tend to disapprove of people who make no secret of the delight they take in sex.

The ancients believed that if a man spent too much of his time 'spilling his seed' the virtue and strength would go out of him. The modern Chinese, with their rigorous work ethic and stern sanctions on pre-marital sex and early marriage, subscribe to much the same view. Other cultures believe that if a man does not have sex often enough his strength will ebb away.

Now, without going overboard and insisting that sex is the only thing which counts in life, because it is not, we do want to see it established as something that is integral and important in most people's lives. It is an odd fact about sex that, here it is, supposed to be one of the most natural functions a human being can perform and yet so many of us find it extremely difficult to consider it in any way naturally.

There are those who elevate it to the status of a sacrament, imbuing it with so much mystery and holiness that it is forthwith transformed into something you cannot talk about, except in hushed tones, and the idea of untouchability, surely the total antithesis of anything to do with sex, also creeps in. 'With my body I thee worship' are beautiful words in their literal meaning, but so much else of the Church's teaching about sex implies that actually moving out of a kneeling position with hands joined in prayer to touching those secret private parts either of your own body or your lover's, borders on defilement and outrage. Very often, sex is an expression of love between two people and they may find that their bodies are saying things to each other which are beyond words, but much of the time sex is simply the normal pleasurable activity of a healthy animal. What happens when people do confuse sex with spirituality can be seen in some of the writings of the mystics. Saint Teresa of Avila, for instance, was a remarkable woman who would have been deeply shocked and horrified if anyone in those pre-Freudian days had suggested to her that what she was really doing was transmuting her orgasmic dreams into paeons of praise for her divine Lover, but that is in fact what she was describing, in beautiful language verging on the erotic.

Another harmful consequence of endowing sex with spiritual significance is that, when it is not sanctified by ritual and prayer and strays outside a rigid dogmatic code of behaviour, it may be condemned as dirty and degrading. The traditional white wedding with modestly veiled bride supported on her father's arm is fraught with sexual symbolism which may be more honoured in the breach than in the observance these days, but many of the prohibitions linger on, even if they are not openly enforced.

Virginity, and its loss, still troubles many women, and men. There is a feeling that whatever you do before marriage, sex sanctified by the matrimonial vows is somehow different, more pure. Even when mystical beliefs are left out, the kid glove manner in which so many children are introduced to the facts of life – 'hush, hush, little ones, a very wonderful thing happens . . .' – often has quite the reverse of the desired effect. How many children have not been appalled or disgusted or frankly disbelieving when the truth has been revealed, possibly by parents or teachers who are themselves insecure in their sexual attitudes or simply downright ignorant. It comes as no surprise that many children grow up with the muddled idea that sex is, at the same time, dirty, forbidden and mysterious, when all they may have ever heard, apart from embarrassed, incomplete explanations, are smutty jokes or horror stories about VD and unwanted pregnancies.

The opposing but no more desirable attitude towards sex is to regard it as some kind of challenge to one's gymnastic abilities. Sexual athletes, who boast of their prowess and rate their success by the number of orgasms they achieve or produce in their partner, have an equally limited and limiting view of sex. Sex is not an olympiad where the high scorers are the ones who make it most often with the most partners and swear that it is sublime every time.

Mature, experienced lovers who are at ease with their bodies and, therefore, with themselves, have realistic expectations about sex. They know that it is not marvellous every time. They know that sometimes they will feel tired or not in the mood, but that even so it is good to be with a lover and perhaps do no more than touch each other gently or cuddle up.

If you remember, we said at the end of the last chapter that the erection a man gets when he is aroused by a woman belongs to her and that she, in the excitement and pleasure she communicates to the man because of the pleasure he is giving her, is in a sense also giving back to him his erection. He makes her feel like a woman and she makes him feel like a man. Therefore, what men and women require from their love-making is that it be reliable and certain and strong. The most intense sexual pleasure and the best is centred in the genital organs, although it is perfectly possible to have good sex without orgasm and without penetration on some occasions. What matters above all for good sex is that we know how to look, to touch and to feel, to ask and to give, and to explore our own and our lover's body. It is also very important that we should be able to talk sexually, not just about the good feelings we experience but also about the times when things are not working out well. A good cook is flattered when he or she is complimented on their skills; indeed more than half their pleasure comes from seeing other people enjoy the results. A good lover similarly likes to be a good giver.

In Sexpiece 1 we asked you to put aside some quiet solitary time just for yourself so that you could luxuriate in a warm bath and touch yourself lovingly all over. You were learning to give to yourself, and you extended this skill in Sexpiece 9. Now we want you to concentrate once more on yourself, but this time with a much more specific end in view. We want you to discover ways of pleasing your partner so that you can enjoy the feeling of being a skilful lover. Either you can ask your lover to demonstrate what is wanted, including masturbation; or you can give your lover the pleasuring that you think is desired and will be found enjoyable, making sure all the time that you are giving what is wanted. This involves the whole of the body including the sex organs.

The one thing that none of us can actually show another person is how to complete the act of intercourse. The best we can do is to learn to give what the other person can teach us they want – and when both of us are giving, both of us are getting. However, before we commit ourselves to intercourse, we can discover ways of being certain that we really do understand what it is our lover requires for satisfaction. In Sexpiece 16 we shall be asking you to learn the skills of mutual masturbation.

Most of us feel very ambivalent about masturbation. Some people have been doing it all their lives, or as long as they can remember, but although they enjoy it and have dismissed the anxieties induced in them by other people – for instance, notions that it is sinful or that it could be harmful by driving them mad or blind or, if they are men, eventually make them impotent – it is still not something to which they openly admit. Masturbation is usually regarded as second best, something you fall back on if for some reason you are without a partner or cannot satisfy your sexual desires in the 'normal' way. The idea that masturbation could be a valuable positive activity in itself and that it can actually heighten the pleasures of love-making with a lover, as well as providing marvellous solace for the times when you are alone or your lover is not feeling sexy, is still not widely accepted.

Both men and women are prey to these inhibitions and it would be invidious to suggest that it is easier for one sex than the other to overcome them. However, we must recognize that there are certain differences between men and women which derive from two factors: their physiological constitution and their psychological conditioning. Both undoubtedly affect their attitudes towards masturbation and their practice of it.

Men tend to be more aware of their genitalia and have been from an earlier age for one very obvious reason: they can see their sexual organs, they can feel them and they are immediately aware of what is happening to them when they are sexually aroused. The penis and testicles hang down outside the body and when a man is sexually excited he not only feels it, he has visible evidence of what is happening to his body by seeing his penis stiffen, enlarge and become erect. He will have been aware of these changes and the feelings which accompany them since he was a young child and, because they are pleasurable, he will, sooner or later, more or less successfully, suppress his emotions of guilt in order to enjoy the sensations he can so easily arouse in himself. He may still think, however, that it betokens a shameful weakness in himself and that it is something to keep to himself because indulging in masturbation is 'not allowed' under the accepted sexual code; on the other hand, the pleasure he gains from bringing himself to climax usually outweighs his cultural or moral scruples. Also, he has been brought up to believe that as a male he has urgent sexual needs which must be gratified and therefore, if he cannot find relief through intercourse with a woman, then masturbation is a possible, even if not altogether desirable, alternative.

It is not so easy for women to overcome their scruples. For one thing, the female sex organs, unlike those of the male, are not immediately visible, apart from the outer lips (labia majora). Both the clitoris and the vagina are concealed and many women are really not quite sure where they are. Then too, they may have been told from an early age that it is not nice to touch themselves down there. If they have not used tampons, perhaps because their mothers have never done so and have passed on their attitude to their daughters that it is a bit disgusting and possibly dangerous to stick things up themselves, they may never touch themselves anywhere between their legs except for basic hygiene. Such women will certainly not have touched themselves exploratively or to give themselves pleasure, but it is only by learning *what* it is that gives you pleasure and *how* to arouse that pleasure that you will be able to ask your lover to please you. As we have said already this is what is meant by taking sexual responsibility for yourself.

Now we are going to suggest practical ways of learning to take on this responsibility fully, both for your own sake and in order to please your lover who will be telling you as you tell him or her what it is that gives them pleasure. Sexually, the source of the most intense pleasure is in the genitals, so we are going to ask you to concentrate on this part of your body especially now.

Sexpiece 16

Start by pleasuring each other in all the ways you have already been doing – running your hands over your lover's body, gently stroking, rubbing and caressing each other. Do not make the mistake of lying side by side because that immediately hinders your freedom of movement; one arm is likely to be pinioned under your body, and you will be unable to see what is happening either to your own body or your lover's as both of you become increasingly aroused.

As you feel your body responding to your lover's touch, try and concentrate your awareness, not so much on what your body is doing but on what the underlying sensations mean to you. For instance, if you are a man your penis will begin to grow and swell and stiffen as your lover gently strokes it and you guide her fingers to circle it and press and rub where it is most exquisitely sensitive. If you are a woman, and your lover inserts his fingers gently between your labia and starts to search in a rhythmic circling manner for your clitoris, you will feel your lips swell and part and your vagina will feel moist and warm. Both of you should let these genital reactions engulf you while concentrating on the pleasure that they produce in you. As they establish themselves and you shut everything else out of your mind, you will feel them deepening and intensifying because you are surrendering yourself to them and thus heightening your physical receptivity.

Your brain as well as your body is fully engaged on just one thing – increasing your sexual pleasure – and you will find that the psychological stimulation induced by thinking about ways of making that pleasure grow has a stimulating effect on your body as well. Mind and body interact on each other in an expanding cycle of pleasure.

Now lie still and quiet for a while. Let the physical and psychological stimulations die down and you will feel the genital sexual feelings you have been enjoying slipping away until once more you feel ready to be aroused or to arouse yourself. •

Here are some more detailed suggestions about ways for each of you to give the other more intense genital sensation. Decide between you who is going to do the deliberate arousing first and, before you start, have some body lotion or KY jelly at hand, because although the woman's body responds to sexual excitement by secretions from the vagina, the clitoris reacts in the same way as the penis. As both organs become engorged with blood they stiffen and enlarge, but neither has any natural lubrication and can become very sore if there is much friction. The last thing either of you want is pain in your love-making, so use saliva and vaginal secretions but, if necessary, supplement them by rubbing yourselves or each other with the lotion.

The woman

If it is the man to begin the pleasuring, then you (woman) lie on your back and open your legs so that he can kneel between them and look at you. He will start by gently massaging you round your hips and thighs. Slowly his hands will move inwards and caress the soft inner side of your thighs. As you begin to feel warm and receptive you should encourage him by showing him with your eyes and your words, or simply by murmuring appreciatively – whatever comes most naturally to you – how his actions are exciting and pleasing you. Then, as your feelings become more localized in your genitals, let yourself luxuriate in the warmth and moisture you begin to feel flowing out of your vagina. When the lips, enclosing your vagina, part and you long for more intense stimulation, take his hand and guide his fingers to find and stroke your clitoris. Talk to each other all the time. You will know where your clitoris is by locating the most pleasurable sensations just above your vaginal opening. Just follow your feelings and your lover must learn to give you the touching *you* want, in the way you want it and where you want it.

As we explained earlier, many women stop themselves from following their own feelings, either because they think it is immodest or improper to ask for pleasure, or because they have been brainwashed into thinking that the man always knows best. In fact, he very seldom does, unless he is a remarkably sensitive and experienced lover in which case he is more likely to want to be told by his lover exactly what pleases her most, because his experience will have taught him that no two women are alike in their sexual needs and responses. However, the majority of men, often because they too are victims of the conditioning which says that it is a man's duty to assume the responsibility of taking charge in lovemaking, go through the same motions time after time with the same partner or with different ones, without ever stopping to ask themselves whether what they are doing is what their partner really wants.

Now the time has come to unlearn this conditioning and apply your new sexual understanding in practice. There is, for instance, a common delusion among men that women are sexually stimulated by the same sensations which excite men. Since a man knows for himself that hard rhythmic rubbing of his penis, gradually increasing in speed and intensity leads him into a mounting crescendo of sexual excitement which will finally culminate in his climax, he believes that a woman is similarly excited by strong, repetitive rubbing. The woman who is true to herself and true to her own feelings knows, however, that the sensations leading her to climax are far more subtle and varied and complex than this. She usually prefers gentle, probing, almost fluttery touching which only gradually, and not always, becomes more insistent and regular. All the way through to climax she may want to be led to small peaks of excitement and then pause as if she were climbing a mountain to enjoy the scenery before being led on and up again to the next peak by her feelings and her lover's sensitive searching lips and fingers. Although we have stressed the importance of psychological stimulation – the mind involved in directing the body – it must not be allowed to take over to the extent of imposing preconceived ideas about how you ought to be touched or what you ought to be feeling. The only right way in love-making is the way which feels right for you and that may have very little to do with anything you have ever been taught to expect. This is true for both men and women.

When the woman has been satisfied by the pleasure her lover has given her, which may or may not have led her to climax – more about this later – it becomes the turn of her man to be pleasured.

The man

Start in the same way with you (man) lying on your back, your legs spread apart and the woman kneeling between them. She starts by massaging your hips and thighs, gradually moving inwards as you did for her. Then let her play with your balls and your penis. Let her cradle your balls gently in her hand and run her fingers softly up and down the raised seam of skin which runs between them down to your back passage. Show her how to stroke your penis and slide her hands up and down the shaft, and tell her with your eyes and your voice how you feel as her hands bring your penis to life, so that she can share your pride and delight and experience her power over you. Show her exactly where your penis feels most sensitive on the underside just below the knob and teach her to touch you there in the way you enjoy most. Follow your feelings and your inclinations and show her what to do in the way that she did with you. Remember what we said about the clitoris and the penis not providing their own natural lubrication, so make sure that you have some cream or body lotion near at hand. Nothing will turn you off more than feeling sore and inflamed just as you find yourself wanting more and more of the same sensation.

Sometimes it is easier to help your lover understand how to touch you genitally by touching yourself and showing exactly how you like it. If you have not done this before you may feel a little embarrassed or find that irrelevant thoughts are invading your mind, such as wondering what your parents or friends would think of you if they saw you now. Dismiss them before they assume any shape or size by recognizing them for the child-based inhibitors that they are. You no longer have to answer to anyone but your lover for who you are or what you want – both of you – so just think of yourselves and the present immediate sensations that you are giving one another.

Banish any lingering hang-ups you may still harbour that sex which pleases you is in some way dirty or degrading. There is, however, a cardinal rule in love-making never to force either yourself or your lover to do anything contrary to their wishes. Go slow. There will always be another time and another mood when something which seemed strange before now seems absolutely right. Be patient and wait for that moment. If this first time you cannot quite bring yourself to masturbate in front of your lover, then say so quite openly, explaining that you would prefer to wait, perhaps to gain a little more confidence in yourself by practising on your own.

It is almost certain that Sexpiece 16 will lead to Sexpiece 17.

Sexpiece 17

Sexpiece 17 is removing the ban on intercourse. Have fun! •

9. What makes sex go wrong and how do we know?

Now you realize how much is going on during arousal and response and how finely tuned our bodies are, it perhaps will come as less of a surprise to learn that sex does not always work as well as it might do, even for those people who generally derive a good deal of satisfaction and pleasure from sex. So many people simply do not know how their bodies work or how to use them – their own and their partner's – to the best sexual advantage. Bad sex is like any other bad habit: the more a couple persist in doing the wrong things the more difficult it becomes to unlearn them and to accept that it may even be necessary to start almost from the beginning as if they were quite new to the experience. It is not just a matter of unlearning bad physical habits. Bad sex has a bad effect on the whole of a relationship, especially when the couple find it difficult to express their dissatisfaction for fear of hurting their partner or do not know or do not dare to communicate their needs, either verbally or physically.

If you are feeling pleased about the work you have done together and by yourselves up to Sexpiece 14 then you will understand from your own experience what we are saying here.

To be able to enjoy pleasurable intimacy with another person requires thought and understanding and an imaginative appreciation of particular needs at a particular moment. Happily, sexual satisfaction does not invariably depend on completing sexual intercourse. Sometimes one or other of you will be wanting comfort and warmth and sympathy rather than an extended fireworks display. Go back to the cooking analogy for a moment and think how sated you would feel if you had an elaborately cooked and served four-course dinner every night of the year. Apart from the physical effort involved in preparing and digesting such a feast, it does not suit our bodies to be overloaded with rich food. They become bloated, fat and eventually unhealthy. Much the same applies to our sexual feasting. Too much of it on too grand and elaborate a scale and the whole thing is in danger of becoming a turn-off. Our physical appetites, whether for eating or for sex, vary according to our individual temperament, but for most of the time we require the simple luxury of good plain cooking. Little and often is a better recipe for successful sex, as it is for healthy eating, than it is to nourish extravagant expectations of lavish indulgence which too often cannot be met.

It is possible for some couples who have been married a long time to decide that sex is no longer necessary to them because other elements of their relationship more than compensate for this lack; others, if their marriage is exceptionally open and tolerant, may be able to accept that each of them can look elsewhere for sexual fulfilment without this disturbing their own relationship. However, it is more probable that when a couple finds that they are going off sex together they believe that their whole relationship is affected by this declining interest. Usually they are right in this assumption.

The immediate reaction of most people who find themselves in this unhappy situation is to make excuses and lay the blame on someone or something. *My mother never told me/always told me . . . Men need it more than women . . . Why does she lie there like a sack of potatoes? I can't help it if I'm frigid. She makes me feel I'm crude. He makes me feel like a tart. There must be something wrong with me/him/her . . .* and so on. Repeat anything often enough and you can convince yourself of its truth. Yet most sexual difficulties are more easily capable of solution than people give themselves credit for.

We have several times talked about the need to accept responsibility for ourselves sexually. This means being able to say aloud what we think about our bodies, what we like and do not like, and how we feel about our lover's body; it means being ready to do the same for our lover without either feeling offended or slighted or bashful. Making love well is neither a guessing game nor a game of chance but it can still be full of surprises if we can only let ourselves be led by our desires and not by our prejudices. If we can genuinely accept sexual responsibility for ourselves we will also be more ready to look for the real cause of trouble, should it arise, instead of seeking escape by fault-finding, which invariably leads to a build-up of resentment, despair and, at its most destructive, bitterness. Couples who allow these feelings to fester within themselves rather than dispersing them by talking them out or, if the situation has got very bad, by seeking help from an experienced third party like a marriage counsellor or a sex therapist, or a book like this, will soon find themselves in deeply troubled waters to the point that they may decide the marriage has broken down beyond any hope of restructuring it. While we are hardly so naïve as to suggest that every match between a man and woman is meant to last for ever or even that it can be maintained on a satisfactory keel all the time, we do believe that many people give up, not because they do not want to resolve their differences but because they have no idea how to set about so doing.

Anything physical or psychological – illness, fatigue, worry, anger, to name but a few – can affect our sexual functioning. Often the effect is quite fleeting and we hardly notice it in the ups and downs of our daily life, but should it intrude upon our notice it may become a cause of worry. We can then get caught up in a vicious circle where worrying about the problem that we want to put right just makes it worse. All the sexpieces that you have done so far and the understanding of your own physical and psychological processes that you have developed by doing them should make the following observation blindingly obvious: namely, that it is the right of a healthy body to respond sexually and that the sexual responses of our bodies are naturally pleasurable. Unlike animals, however, human beings can get very fouled-up with the way they manage their feelings and the way they think. Our mind is so closely related to our body that our psychological life can affect our physical and, most especially, our sexual life.

Many processes go on quite naturally and automatically in the body. Our hearts beat. Our stomachs start the digestive process and our bowels finish it off. Without these processes working properly we become ill and may easily die. Curiously enough, our sexual function is one of these same natural processes but it is the only one in our physical system which can be completely impaired by our psychological processes throughout the whole of our adult life without death resulting. For the man who turns his anxiety into a peptic ulcer, or his worry into a heart attack – problems unknown to animals in their natural state except under conditions of the most intense fear – considerable pain and often prolonged surgery and patching up, if not death, are the consequences. Yet the man whose anxiety turns into impotence is the unkind butt of music hall jokes. Lives can be crippled by bad sex.

This chapter contains a number of case histories illustrating various disorders. You may or may not find your particular difficulty exactly mirrored as there are always particular circumstances for producing the same problem. However, if you read this chapter carefully and then look at the treatment chart at the end, you should be able to identify your problem and proceed to whichever of the subsequent chapters deals with it in detail.

It is important to remember that just as, generally speaking, sex happens between two people, it takes two to have a sexual problem and two to resolve it. Even when it appears completely one-sided as in the case of a woman who complains that she never has an orgasm whereas her man climaxes perfectly satisfactorily every time, the reason why she is non-orgasmic may have as much to do with the way he approaches her and handles her as her own attitudes. Almost everything we have asked you to do so far we have asked you to do together, and this becomes more than ever important when you attempt to deal with the particular difficulty you are encountering in your sex life.

There are four major types of sexual disorder, two for men and two for women, which directly affect one or other of the two stages in the sexual cycle of arousal and climax. There are also disorders affecting penetration which are to do with the mechanics of making love and difficulties associated with low levels of sexual interest.

We shall deal first with *disorders of arousal*.

In a man sexual arousal is evidenced when he has an erection but if, for some reason, and despite his feeling sexually excited and wanting to have intercourse, the blood does not pump into his penis, he will not get an erection. This has generally been called *impotence*, but because this wrongly suggests general weakness it is more accurate, if somewhat clumsy, to call it erectile insufficiency: the erection is not strong enough for effective penetration.

Case History 2: Dorothy and John

Difficulty: simple impotence – mid-life work stress. At the time of therapy Dorothy and John were both aged forty-seven. John is a skilled fitter in a car factory, Dorothy has not worked since marriage and they have an only, much loved daughter Jeanette, aged nine, for whom they had to wait much longer than they expected. They are buying their own house on a mortgage which they took out when they married twenty-five years ago.

Dorothy had been urging John for the past three years to move house and the pressures had increased since he had recently been made a foreman. Dorothy wanted more garden and a better school for Jeanette, but John was finding his new job more difficult than he had expected and he was worried by some unfavourable comments he had received from his manager. All in all, he was feeling a bit near the limit of his resources and he was sure that a new mortgage was more than he could support comfortably.

'Comfortable' was the word they both used to describe their love-making. In the past nine months John had had increasing difficulty getting an erection and Dorothy was feeling neglected. Both had begun to wonder if John was getting a bit past it now, but Dorothy said she was missing sex and persuaded John to seek help through his family doctor.

Resolution. Both John and Dorothy were each other's first and only sexual relationship. They had never made love with the light on, with their night clothes off, or anywhere but in bed.

During the sensate focus of Sexpieces 10 and 11 John began to experience strong spontaneous erections which he learnt to let come and go in response to the changing stimulation of the session. Both enjoyed making love with no clothes on but they remained shy of keeping the lights on.

They decided not to move house and instead they bought a new car so that they could enjoy longer week-end trips as a family. •

There are several varieties of erectile insufficiency. The story of Dorothy and John illustrates the most common, which is the gradual loss of firm erections over a period of time in mid-life. In this particular case, it was associated with increasing work stress, but other reasons could include depression about the onset of middle age, severe financial worries, redundancy, etc.

Another not uncommon variety is where a man has never, on any occasion throughout his life since sexual maturation, maintained an erection sufficiently strong for insertion. In the following case history this was caused by a single, traumatic first attempt at intercourse in unfavourable circumstances.

Case History 3: Arthur and Mavis

Difficulty: impotence – primary type, i.e. no successful penetration. Arthur is a storeman in a meat factory and his thin, sad appearance contrasted strongly at his first visit with that of Mavis, his wife, a jolly woman who works as a shop assistant. Aged thirty and twenty-three respectively, they came for treatment after three years of marriage.

They had met at a dance hall where Mavis had asked Arthur for a dance on a dare from one of her friends. He always went to dances, but he seldom got up and he never felt he could ask the same girl twice because he never knew what to say after the usual opening remarks. Since, however, Mavis had made the first approach he did manage to suggest, 'It's my turn to ask now'. She had accepted and so it continued all evening, each taking turns to ask the other.

Courting lasted six months. Mavis liked his steady ways – her father had been something of a drinker. Arthur liked her laugh and good humour. His mother had died when he was seven and his father had looked after him as best he could but the home had always seemed cold. Mavis had made love a few times before she met Arthur, but he had only tried once – disastrously – with a prostitute. When he had gone to her room the woman had masturbated him very quickly to climax and then asked for her money. Arthur had been humiliated and confused.

On their honeymoon Mavis started fondling Arthur's penis, whereupon he was flooded with the same feelings he had had with the prostitute. However, no erection came and Mavis was puzzled. They did not try again for a month but meanwhile Arthur masturbated to reassure himself that he was all right. Finding that he could masturbate he then began to fear his next contact with Mavis. He felt guilty about getting an erection by himself so when Mavis asked him if he had ever come he replied that he had never masturbated. Quite soon, the fear of failure made Arthur totally unable to relax sexually in Mavis's presence.

Resolution. Sexpieces 4 to 8 freed Arthur from his guilt about his body and enabled him to enjoy Mavis's warmth without worrying about 'performing'. Sexpiece 9 taught him how to enjoy masturbating himself and this time he knew both that Mavis knew what he was doing and that she knew he knew about her learning to pleasure herself, which in fact she had never done before. Erections in Mavis's presence began to get stronger and more frequent, and they both enjoyed them.

At the end of treatment their love-making was very gentle. Arthur enjoys 'quiet vagina' exercises especially but he understands that Mavis would like him to let go a bit more. Both are convinced that it will happen in time. •

Case History 4: Bill and Sue

Difficulty: impotence known as anapriapism – erection disappears at moment of insertion. Bill and Sue found that Bill's erection disappeared just as they were about to make love. No matter how excited they both were and how strong Bill's erection, time after time during their love-making Sue was left feeling frustrated and Bill felt a failure. After two years of sex becoming less and less frequent they had a blazing row and Sue left the flat they shared. Bill promised to see what could be done to help if she would come back. They arrived for their first appointment separately. She was angry. He was hurt.

History-taking by the therapists for the next hour and a half revealed nothing very unusual about Bill's experiences. They did establish, however, that he had once made love as a teenager and that afterwards the girl had told Bill she thought he had made her pregnant. He knew that his parents would be furious and he did not want to marry her but he started laying plans for leaving school at the end of his first year in the sixth form and getting work of any description. After eight weeks of anxiety the girl had a period.

Bill did not sleep with another girl until his final year in college when he started living with Sue. He knew that she had had boy-friends before and that she used a contraceptive cap but he had never seen one until she stopped their first love-making to put one in, together with some spermicidal cream. He was not quite sure how it worked in the vagina but he worried that the method seemed clumsy and not very safe. He had heard that sheaths were not too reliable either and wondered if Sue would take the pill, but he did not like to ask her, particularly now that he was having trouble with his erections. Anyway he made no connections be-tween his subconscious fears of making her pregnant and his ear-lier experience which he had done his best to forget, especially after one of his friends did make the same girl pregnant the next year and left school to marry her.

Resolution. Sexpieces 12 and 13 were especially useful to Bill and Sue. She discovered just how little Bill knew about a woman's body and then realized that she was not too knowledgeable herself. He was very reassured when Sue handled his penis and talked about it to him and then learnt to masturbate him in Sexpiece 16 and enjoy his climax.

Many men are vaguely worried about what happens inside the vagina, just as many women are concerned that if something as large as an erect penis comes inside them, it will cause damage. (See Case History 13.) These anxieties and fears prevent the normal sexual reflexes of arousal and climax from working effectively and, for a few men like Bill, it means they switch off at just the wrong moment.

In this particular instance, the causes were not too difficult to establish but sometimes a case like this needs more protracted treatment like psychotherapy which involves deeper probing into the causes. •

Just as the term impotence is beginning to go, the term frigid is also rapidly losing favour, and a good thing too. Helen Singer Kaplan[5] prefers the term 'general sexual dysfunction' to describe the woman who does not experience pleasure from sexual stimulation. Again this is clumsy but at least it does not make any disparaging suggestions about a woman's temperament. A woman who is unaroused sexually does not lubricate from her vagina nor does she show other signs, like erect nipples or an overall mottled skin flush which are all due to increased blood flow engorging special blood vessels. As with erectile insufficiency in the man, the difficulty might have been there always or only occur later in a woman's sexual life, due to a particular cause or situation.

Case History 5: Jane and Jack

Difficulty: situational loss of arousal in a woman. Jane and Jack had been lovers for two years before their marriage and although they had not lived together and the opportunities for love-making had been infrequent, when they were together they had been very aroused and easily reached climax. They had taken two holidays together when they made love as often as possible.

When they returned from their honeymoon they moved into a new house. Jack went back to his job as a draughtsman and Jane found work in a travel agency. They were living in Jack's home town and he spent two nights a week out with his old friends while Jane caught up on the household chores. When they were together, Jack would occasionally help with the washing-up but it depended what was on television and most nights he stayed up watching to the end. Jane would go to bed before him, saying she felt too tired the next day if she was not asleep by half past ten.

Gradually sex became the last event of the day. Sometimes Jack woke Jane up; sometimes he wanted a quickie in the morning. Jane began to feel deeply resentful and intercourse became painful for her. After nine months of marriage they were quarrelling all the time.

The combination of Jane's tiredness, induced by coping with a new job, a new house, a man to look after full-time and sex at the end of the day, plus her increasing disappointment followed by dull anger that Jack was not as attentive as he had been before marriage and that he had reverted to many of his bachelor habits, caused Jane's arousal process to switch off. It was not long before Jack's attempts to penetrate her caused actual pain because she had not even started to lubricate.

Resolution. Deciding to work together on the sexpieces meant that they had to make time for each other and they very quickly learnt how easy it is to forget about private time for sexual pleasures in a marriage. They found all the sexpieces interesting and they learnt new information about how their bodies function but, above all, it was this making time for one another that set their love-making back on to the spontaneous and pleasurable track it had been before they married. •

There is a related condition, known as sexual anaesthesia, where a woman shows all the physical signs of being sexually stimulated: her vagina lubricates, swells and changes in colour, her breasts change shape and her nipples stand out, but she herself feels no pleasurable stimulus whatever. You could describe her as being numb because although her physical mechanism is in sound working order her experience of what is happening to her is completely blocked off.

Case History 6: Mary

Difficulty: sexual anaesthesia. Mary came to the clinic on her own. She had had boyfriends since the age of seventeen and now, five years later, was thinking about getting engaged, but she was worried that while she liked men and particularly appreciated her current man who was ten years older than her and generous and kind, she could not find any pleasure in physical contact. It did not repel her. She just could not see what the fuss was about and felt that 'down there' on both men and women was rather messy. She had never had intercourse nor had she seen a man's erect penis.

However, talking with Mary established the fact that she did experience wetness between her legs if there was a lot of kissing and petting. And this worried her. She felt it might stain her skirt if it seeped through her pants and she felt awkward when washing between her legs later. Stickiness was a sensation she had never liked. Like her mother, Mary was very houseproud and fastidious; she always wore rubber gloves for preparing messy foods like raw meat or fish and when washing up. She also disliked putting on face creams.

It was clear that Mary did physically have an arousal, but mentally she felt nothing of the sensations in her pelvis at all. Her body reacted appropriately to stimulation but she did not feel it reacting.

Resolution: Mary worked through her sexpieces on her own in so far as a partner was not needed. She began to enjoy bathing as a place to dream and luxuriate and she tried out different bath oils and body lotions. Her boyfriend was delighted by her new scented freshness.

She found Sexpiece 9 very important and found Betty Dodson's book on masturbation very helpful.[6] She thought carefully about Sexpiece 10 and started wondering how she would enjoy being in bed with her man. She left treatment certain that she now knew how to pleasure herself and to develop her physical relationship with her boyfriend who had become her fiancé. (He thought that he was responsible for the change in Mary because, at that stage, he had not yet learnt that a woman does not actually need a man to turn her on; having a man is just one of the ways.) •

Sometimes disorders of arousal are selective. A man may be capable of intercourse with a prostitute but not his wife, and a woman may be aroused by a lover but not her husband.

Case History 7: Sally and David

Difficulty: selective response. Sally was married to David who was struggling to become an accountant. He had got rather stuck working for his finals and worried about the future.

He had had an unhappy childhood and his parents had separated when he was fourteen. Living with his mother he had become the man of the house, spending more time with her than with friends. His father was an accountant and his mother felt it was a secure profession. She brought David up to be thrifty and prudent. She was clearly displeased about David's swift marriage to Sally who was a year older than him.

Sally's parents had been ambitious for her but she left school at fifteen, became a secretary and wanted to get married before she was twenty-two. She was not far off this age when David appeared. Her father, who had some difficulty settling down after National Service, had been a travelling salesman among many other, quite brief, jobs. Her mother always made the best of every situation and both parents had a happy-go-lucky attitude towards money, spending what they had and never saving.

Neither Sally nor David had had steady partners before and they did not sleep together before marriage. They went to live with his mother.

Sally had learnt to masturbate from an article she had once read in *Forum* magazine. Although she felt rather guilty about doing it she enjoyed it and knew what an orgasm was from her own experience.

David maintained his erection and did not ejaculate too quickly, but he was unimaginative in his love-making and found it difficult to let himself go. Try as they might, Sally could not reach a climax with David.

In due course she had a brief affair with a man who came into the office to repair the typewriters. She was wildly orgasmic during intercourse with her lover and wondered if she ought to leave David or stay with him for at least the home he could provide when qualified.

Resolution. Sally visited a marriage guidance counsellor by herself and then went for sex therapy. She began to understand more about herself and why she had so much hope invested in David. She realized that her disappointment in his difficulty over qualifying was blocking any other positive feelings she had about him. She also saw that there was a connection between her pleasurable guilt at masturbating to climax and the guilt of her affair. Furthermore, the mechanic with whom she had had the affair had been rather like her father and very unlike David and she then understood that she missed her father's cheerful nature even if he did sometimes conceal money worries.

During the sex therapy Sally told David that she was not enjoying her sex life with him as much as she would like. He was not altogether surprised because he had wondered but had not dared to ask her. She taught him to be the lover that she wanted and he responded by being more spontaneous and, therefore, effective.

He passed his finals and Sally concluded the treatment feeling that by doing something good for herself she had also done something good for David. •

Here is another example of selective loss of response which in this case refers to a woman but can happen as easily to a man.

Case History 8: June and Jim

Difficulty: loss of response. June found a letter in Jim's pocket from a girl he had met on a sales trip which made it clear that they had slept together. She felt overwhelmed by anger and hurt but did not dare confront Jim as she feared his possibly violent reaction. Previously they had enjoyed sex; he had usually called the tune and she had responded and if, on occasion, she felt less enthusiastic than him, she had always been happy to please him. Sometimes she did think it might be fun to be a little more experimental, but then reminded herself that she was grateful for twenty years of marriage, her home and the two boys.

After discovering his infidelity she lapsed into depression which scared Jim who took her to the doctor and insisted that she take the pills prescribed. Although deep down Jim loved June, he had been taking her for granted for years and sometimes felt annoyed with her for being so dependent on him. June kept the reasons for her unhappiness to herself and Jim did not dare allow himself to speculate on them. He wondered fleetingly if she had found the letter because he remembered asking her to take the jacket to the cleaners, but then banished the idea as he felt sure she would have said something if she had.

After a while her depression improved and Jim resumed his casual ways whereupon she became depressed once more. One evening he criticized her for the untidy state of the house and she responded by bursting into tears and pouring out her rage and humiliation. Jim, who had managed to put the whole episode of his affair behind him, was aghast and remorseful. Neither slept much that night but over the following weeks they talked things out and both felt that they could cope with the situation. June stopped taking her anti-depressants and Jim no longer dreaded coming home each night.

Love-making started again, but June found she could not let go. She felt as if she was doing it just to please him and sub-consciously she no longer trusted him. Jim began to wonder what was wrong with him.

Resolution. After a year of this unsatisfactory love-making, when they had reached the point of blaming each other and thinking seriously about separation, they came for sex therapy.

The therapists wondered if the couple needed marital psycho-therapy rather than sex therapy and discussed the matter with them, but both said they would prefer to try and remedy the sexual part of their relationship as that seemed to be the immediate cause of trouble.

It was the talking in Sexpieces 5 and 6 and the quiet enjoy-ment of 12 and 13, followed by the deeper talking of Sexpiece 14 that they agreed had changed their sex life and gave them a new foundation on which to rebuild their relationship. Using the 'I' language dispelled any notions of blame and both discovered that they could pleasure themselves selfishly without worrying about the other person's feelings. Then they found that they could share their feelings without feeling doubtful about what the other person was not saying. Finally, June became responsive to her own pleasure as well as Jim's.

The treatment ended with a restored marriage and June feeling a new sense of liberation and self-confidence. •

This case is a straightforward example of a woman who is turned off sex for a specific reason. Failure to experience arousal may also be a symptom of declining interest in a particular man, but usually when this happens it is more likely to show itself in a failure to reach orgasm than in a failure to become aroused.

The next set of problems are to do with *disorders of climax*. In the man, one of two things happen: either he comes too quickly – premature ejaculation – or he comes too slowly, or not at all – retarded ejaculation.

Case History 9: Peter and Fay

Difficulty: premature ejaculation. Peter was a virgin until his marriage at the age of twenty-two. He found Fay very attractive and had frequently masturbated while thinking about her. He also had wet dreams in which Fay had been arousing him very deliberately and he awoke with a powerful climax. Occasionally he wondered what she would think if she knew he was masturbating about her and what she would say about his ejaculate. Would she mind the mess?

On their first honeymoon night they were both exhausted and sleeping on a very rough cross-channel ferry. There was no chance to make love but as soon as they reached the hotel they went to bed. Peter was fascinated and scared by finding himself alone with a completely naked Fay who welcomed him warmly, but as soon as his penis touched her inner thigh he ejaculated suddenly and without any expectation of it happening. He apologized and Fay assured him that it did not matter. She suggested that they should cuddle up but Peter could not believe her because it mattered so much to him, so he turned away and went to sleep, tired from the journey, upset with himself and leaving Fay confused.

So began Peter's experience of premature ejaculation. Occasionally he would get just inside her vagina but he continued to come long before she was ready. At first Fay felt disappointed and then she began to feel used. She too had been a virgin until her marriage but although she had not been sure about the details of lovemaking she knew now that she was not being satisfied. Like Peter she had also masturbated before marriage while thinking of him, but without saying anything to each other they both rejected this as wrong inside marriage.

Peter at least had some sexual relief but Fay got increasingly tense and Peter sensed that all she wanted was for him to get it over as quickly as possible. He felt himself to be a nuisance and that his worst fears had been realized: Fay did not like his ejaculate.

Resolution. Doing the sexpieces in sequence took them back to the beginning of their physical relationship, but without the worries this time. They learnt to relax sexually in each other's company, to explore and share their needs, each teaching the other to give. Peter learnt that the time after a climax is a special time for sharing and talking, not humping straight off to sleep. By the time they had reached Sexpiece 16, Fay was more than ready to learn the squeeze technique (see Sexpiece 23) and Peter to let her control his ejaculation, so that they could both enjoy his erection and his come. •

Case History 10: Margaret and Ted

Difficulty: retarded ejaculation. Margaret and Ted were still courting when her sister, who had just had her first baby, was seized by post-natal depression so acutely that she had to go back into hospital for psychiatric treatment. Ted, who had been brought up in an orphanage, appreciated the warmth and affection of Margaret's home life and shared the family's concern about her sister. He was treated like a son and the man of the house by Margaret's mother, who had been widowed when her daughters were young children.

When Margaret and Ted became officially engaged their petting changed to complete love-making. The very first time they had intercourse Margaret warned him to be careful about coming, meaning really that she did not want to become pregnant. She feared what her mother would say and deep down she was desperately worried that she might have the same reaction to childbirth as her sister.

Ted, anxious not to upset anyone, controlled his erection so that the sensation of inevitability leading to ejaculation, which he had known in the orphanage when being masturbated by a friend, never built up. They married and, after three years, he had still never once come inside her. He occasionally had a wet dream but he never masturbated.

Margaret's sister had recovered and had had another baby without the trouble recurring. Margaret began to think it was about time that they started a family so, after another year of hoping, she went to a fertility clinic for tests and Ted accompanied her. He was unable to supply the doctor with a specimen of semen and was, therefore, given a physical examination but nothing could be found to account for the difficulty. He told the doctor that he was still ejaculating in his sleep about once every three months but that he could not remember any dreams associated with these occasions.

Resolution. He came to the clinic as a thin shy man and Margaret did all the talking.

They had to do a great deal of work together, especially up to Sexpiece 8. Ted's feelings were very blocked off and Margaret learnt gradually to change her 'be careful' to 'come on'. For Ted, it was learning to allow sensation in through his penis which was the most difficult stage of all, so conditioned had he become to preventing it and so deprived had he been of close touching in his orphanage upbringing. Touching a small child makes it feel secure and loved while a lack of caring touching leaves a space inside a person which is like a cold fire on a winter's morning. Margaret spent much time learning to kindle Ted's fire. Gradually the lines of his face softened and his eyes began to sparkle.

First he ejaculated by hand, deliberately and consciously, and soon he was able to come easily inside Margaret. Shortly after their treatment ended she became pregnant and she looked forward to caressing and loving Ted's baby in the way that Ted himself had missed so much as a child. •

Failing to establish an orgasm in a woman may lead to vague discomfort and frustration or to intense anger, depression or physical pain. As we described earlier a good deal of blood flows into the soft tissues of the vagina and vulva during arousal and if it is not released by climax can produce a chronic dull ache of the inner thighs and groin.

Case History 11: Alan and Denise

Difficulty: lack of climax. Alan was thirty-one years older than Denise and they got married when she was twenty-one. They had known each other for three years and had fallen in love at their very first meeting. However, Denise's father, who was younger than Alan and had been recently widowed, insisted that they wait until Denise came of age. Neither of them had been in love before and they felt quite guilty about their feelings for each other. He worked as a librarian in the technical information service division of a major engineering company and she was teaching domestic science. After marriage they moved away from the town to a village eight miles distant.

They came for therapy ten years later, giving as their reason Alan's inability to get an erection. Discussion established that it had always been uncertain and further probing revealed that whenever he did feel aroused he tried to use his erection immediately, whereupon it disappeared. Denise admitted that she was feeling frustrated and edgy and, at the age of thirty-one, there was a slight primness in the set of her mouth. Alan had a faintly apologetic air about him.

On the surface they were a happily-married couple, devoted to each other's comfort and well-being, but beneath it they were very miserable about the loneliness at the core of their relationship. Moreover, Denise was experiencing the increased sexual drive normal to a woman in her early thirties while Alan was experiencing the opposite – a slight decline in his levels of sexual activity, appropriate to a man just turned sixty. (There is a difference of course between sexual capability and frequency of activity. A man well over sixty may be an excellent lover in all manner of ways even if the frequency of his wish for intercourse is not as strong as it might be in a man in his twenties.)

The case of Denise and Alan was not helped by the fact that there was nothing in their sexual encounters to encourage arousal. They never made love with the light on, they were always careful to undress separately and they never went into the bathroom together. Cautious and over-concerned for each other, Alan worried about hurting Denise with his penis while she silently longed to make demands on him without showing him up as a failure.

Although she had been saying it did not matter they both knew that it did and so when he hinted that perhaps they ought to do something about their situation, she eagerly made the appointment for sex therapy.

Resolution. The sexpieces came as startling revelations to both of them. At last they were giving themselves permission to enjoy each other, look openly, talk freely, ask and give. His erections came quite spontaneously and they looked like a couple deeply in love. As they talked to the therapists about what was happening, they laughed a lot, like children, showing that when ignorance has been eliminated, real innocence – unaffected pleasure – can take over.

The therapists felt very pleased with themselves and then reminded each other that they were only privileged helpers. It was Denise and Alan who had taken the difficult steps of resolving to find help and working the programme through and not ducking out when the going got hard or seemed over-demanding. The most a therapist can do is to chart the route, but it is the couple themselves who have to walk the road, get miserable when they take the wrong turning and eventually discover that the journey was worthwhile. •

Just as in problems of arousal, a woman can be non-orgasmic most of the time or find that it only happens at a particular period or with a particular person.

Case History 12: George and May

Difficulty: lack of climax. May's second pregnancy coincided with George changing jobs and they moved to a new town. George was under much greater pressure in his new work than he had expected, nor was it quite what he had hoped for. He came home from work feeling fed-up with himself and cross with May who was not coping as well as she had with the first pregnancy. In fact she was not finding things nearly as easy with an active toddler around her all day, getting to know new shops, trying to make new friends and doing her best not to complain about the little time George spared her to sort out the house after the move.

Despite the valid excuses of overwork, George was less supportive and interested than he had been over their first child. Subconsciously he blamed May for getting pregnant again so quickly. It was not that he minded having another child – they had always agreed that they would have two – but he wished its arrival could have been better timed.

Intercourse became infrequent and when it did happen May felt she wanted arousing slowly. She did not always want an orgasm but she did want to feel safe and cherished. George, however, was usually tired and wanted sexual relief rather than extended lovemaking so he came quickly and then turned over to sleep pulling most of the covers with him and leaving May feeling very frustrated. Often she cried herself to sleep.

A vicious circle of feeling angry with both George and herself set up, which was strengthened by George's continued worries about work and his irritability with May for not being the wife he thought he had married.

Resolution. They came for sex therapy eighteen months after the birth of the second child, saying that May had become frigid.

The idea that women are not in themselves frigid, but that they are made unresponsive by their own feelings and those they perceive coming from their partner as well as by lack of knowledge on both sides about how their sexual systems work, physically and psychologically, came as a revelation to both of them.

Sexpieces 10 and 11 were especially helpful for putting them back in touch with each other and reassuring themselves that they were not being rejected because of the extra pressures that had come into both their lives. •

The third set of sexual disorders are connected with penetration or insertion and block effective intercourse. *Vaginismus* in women is a spasm of the lower part of the vaginal barrel which makes the vaginal entrance contract and close in response to the slightest touch, whether from hand, penis or tampon. The muscular reaction is entirely involuntary but its cause is usually rooted in deep anxiety or may be a form of painful memory reflex to a traumatic experience earlier in life, like rape or a grossly clumsy medical examination. This condition is best cured by sex therapy rather than surgical intervention.

Case History 13: Betty and Geoff

Difficulty: vaginismus. Betty and Geoff came for treatment after three years of marriage having first gone to their family doctor to find out why Betty had not become pregnant. When he examined her he soon discovered that she tightened up when he tried to insert a finger into her vagina and, if he pressed slightly, her back arched and she tried to move backwards up the examining table. He diagnosed her tense withdrawal and total rejection of any attempt at insertion as vaginismus.

Betty had always been terrified of anything going into her vagina, especially a penis. She had never used tampons and indeed, as a young girl, had not known that women had periods until she found herself bleeding one night and thought she was bleeding to death. In the dark she had the most vivid and terrifying imaginings, fearing that somehow the lower part of her had burst open. Her mother explained briefly and imprecisely to her in the morning what was happening to her but it was not sufficient to banish the fears and fantasies locked away inside her. She would have liked to know more about what went on inside her body but did not dare to ask her mother and did not know who else to approach.

Geoff was a quiet shy man. He liked petting, but sensed Betty's tenseness the moment he put his hand above her knee so he did not press it and anyway he was not himself very clear about what was involved in love-making.

Resolution. Both Geoff and Betty were profoundly ignorant about how their bodies worked and during their entire marriage had never had proper intercourse. In Sexpiece 10 Betty learnt how to feel positive about her body and in Sexpiece 9 Geoff learnt how to pleasure himself. The sexual information they gained by doing all the sexpieces, but particularly 12 and 13, was vital to them. At last Betty understood how her body worked and this knowledge gave her the courage to explore her vagina with her fingers, eventually letting Geoff also do it for her. Week by week their confidence increased as they took charge of their own bodies instead of being mystified and, in Betty's case, frightened by them. •

Anapriapism in men (see Case History 4) is a similar disorder in men and, like vaginismus, is usually psychological in origin.

The final group of sexual difficulties is the result of low sexual drive which is not yet very well understood. We know it can be dampened down; some drugs have this effect as do certain illnesses and the emotions of fear, anxiety and fatigue. It also seems likely that different people do vary in the level of their sexual drive, but it only becomes a problem in a relationship where the partners have markedly different levels of sexual need and interest.

Almost always the problem is expressed in terms of intercourse. One person wants it much more or less than the other. Such a situation then creates its own tensions and angers until it develops to the point where love-making becomes even more infrequent and less satisfactory.

Case History 14: Wendy and Ray

Difficulty: low sex drive. Wendy and Ray, who had been married for six years, were both in their early thirties. She was a schoolteacher and he was an accountant. They had agreed not to have children.

When they came for treatment Wendy was feeling very frustrated, although Ray was a kind, considerate man, helpful round the house, and often cooking the evening meal and washing it up while she corrected school work. However, he always fell asleep very rapidly when they went to bed and Wendy found herself wishing that there was more life in him, even if only to have a decent row.

Resolution. By doing the sexpieces they both learnt that a person's first sexual responsibility is to themself. Wendy had never thought of masturbating and certainly not of using a vibrator. She learnt to do both and to use her body for her own pleasure.

Now she no longer felt angry with Ray or blamed him for not making love to her to relieve her own sexual tension. Ray found that by no longer being under pressure or feeling obliged to have intercourse, he could relax and really enjoy the occasions when they did. Moreover, now that Wendy was no longer sexually dependent on him he began to see her in a slightly new light and to feel more curious about her sexual arousal. Wendy shared her masturbating with him and he found it surprisingly exciting.

Their love-making became more frequent and the quality of it was much improved. As Wendy became less demanding, Ray became more giving and the hostility they had been feeling towards each other vanished. Once more they appreciated the good qualities which had attracted them to each other in the first place and they no longer felt resentful about their sexual disparity because they had found a satisfactory solution. •

This is a brief description of the main sexual disorders which

Treatment chart

Woman

It concerns me that I	This is what the experts call	We suggest you use this book to Sexpiece 14, then Turn to case histories	And then move on to
don't get sexually aroused	general sexual dysfunction	5, 6, 7	Chapter 11 & Sexpieces 20, 2
get excited but don't reach a climax	orgastic dysfunction	7, 8, 11, 12	Chapter 12 & Sexpiece 22
find my vagina is too tight to let a penis in	vaginismus	13	Chapter 15 & Sexpiece 25
don't seem very interested in sex	low sex drive	14	Chapters 1–8 Sexpieces 1–17

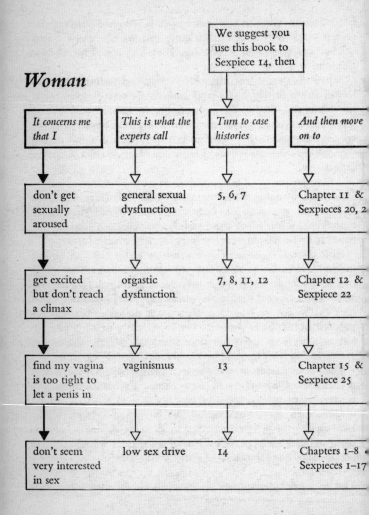

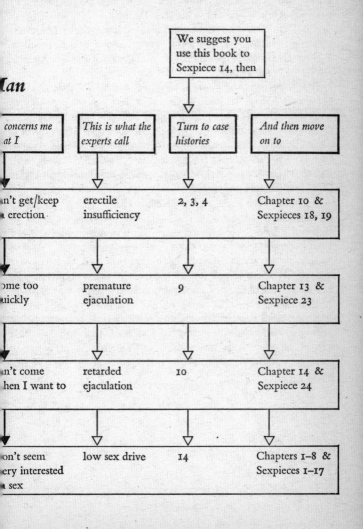

Man

We suggest you use this book to Sexpiece 14, then			
concerns me at I	This is what the experts call	Turn to case histories	And then move on to
n't get/keep a erection	erectile insufficiency	2, 3, 4	Chapter 10 & Sexpieces 18, 19
ome too uickly	premature ejaculation	9	Chapter 13 & Sexpiece 23
n't come hen I want to	retarded ejaculation	10	Chapter 14 & Sexpiece 24
on't seem ery interested a sex	low sex drive	14	Chapters 1–8 & Sexpieces 1–17

people suffer from but, as even our limited selection of case histories shows, the variations and permutations experienced by individuals are considerable. More than one problem can be present in the same relationship and in the same person.

Now turn to pages 116–17 and use the treatment chart to check your own problem – if you think you have one – and then follow it through by reading whichever of the subsequent chapters is relevant to your case.

This is perhaps the moment to repeat our advice that the self-help sex therapy described in this book does not attempt to deal with more than the presenting sexual difficulty which may have its origin in some deeper psychological disturbance. However, it is our experience that sexual difficulties, once they emerge, tend to take on a life of their own, creating new problems in their turn, and that it is often beneficial to the whole relationship to tackle them immediately and directly.

If you both feel that you have made useful progress by working through Sexpieces 1 to 13, then you will certainly be ready to tackle the later, relevant sexpieces. If, however, you have got stuck somewhere before Sexpiece 13 or you have skipped certain of these early sexpieces and you know that you have done the rest imperfectly then do not continue with any more sexpieces. The work up to Sexpiece 13 is absolutely necessary before you move on further. Should you now find yourself completely stuck, which does not mean that you have failed but is a clear indication that you have not yet discovered what you need, then we do advise you to talk to your doctor, a Marriage Guidance Counsellor or to seek out a sex therapist from the information at the back of this book.

10. He can't keep an erection

A man who cannot either keep an erection or get one at all or finds that it is insufficiently firm, fears that he will be impotent for life. Before discussing why it happens – and it is estimated that more than half the male population may suffer from a temporary period of it at some time or other in their lives – let us make sure that we understand what it means to be impotent.

Impotent. The very word strikes a chill. There is a grim suggestion of finality about it, an idea that if he cannot do it once he cannot do it twice, and so on and for ever. Fear and anxiety about his performance are the impotent man's worst enemies. He is not helped by the negative and misleading implications inherent in the word itself and it is for this reason, already touched upon in the last chapter, that we would prefer to talk about erectile insufficiency. However, recognizing the clumsiness of this new definition and the fact that impotence is still the most usual way of describing the problem we shall bow to custom as long as you remember that what we mean by impotence is lack of power in the erection and not lack of power in the man.

Case Histories 2, 3 and 4 illustrated various aspects of this difficulty. We should not dismiss the possibility, however, that the cause could be physical. If you were not able to complete Sexpiece 9 and had no spontaneous erections at all during Sexpieces 10 and 11, then you should consult your doctor and ask for a physical examination. You may be suffering from an illness like diabetes, a hormonal imbalance or some disease affecting your nervous system.

Severe depression or acute stress and fatigue can also make a man impotent, as can certain drugs, which he may be taking for some other condition or to which he is addicted. Finally, there is alcohol which, as the porter said in *Macbeth*, 'provokes the desire but ... takes away the performance'. Probably most men have experienced at least once in their lives the dismal letdown of feeling randy and ready for love-making after an evening of heavy drinking only to find that their penis has been knocked unconscious. Very humiliating, but most men realize fast enough what has caused their temporary impotence and are more careful next time. Here, however, is a cautionary tale for those who are not yet aware of the anti-aphrodisiac effects of too much alcohol.

There was an eager and virile young man who took his bride on a honeymoon to Ireland where he intended to enjoy her, the fishing and the delicious brand of stout for which that country is famous, in that order. Unfortunately, so carried away was he by the last of these three, which he began drinking in copious draughts to give him courage to approach his bride – with disastrous results – that he then took to drinking it in even greater quantities in a vain attempt to drown his sorrows and forget the misery and the shame of it all. He tried a bit of fishing, but even the trout were not rising, and as for his bride, she spent much of her time weeping in her bedroom. A thoroughly unhappy and despairing couple returned home, convinced that their marriage was finished before it had started, but she did persuade him to visit the doctor as, after all, it was so unlike him. Careful cross-examination revealed the truth. The young man has not become a teetotaller but he knows which of the three pleasures he would renounce first: it is certainly not his wife, and he still goes fishing.

As far as physical causes are concerned, you may already know that you are suffering from a certain illness and have been reading this book to see if you can find some way of improving your sex life. If so we are delighted. Firstly, it shows that you care for your partner and the enjoyment of your own body and, secondly, all the sexpieces that you have been engaging in will have helped you learn new ways of relating to your partner, or confirm you in aspects of your relationship that you may have already developed. As we have said before, sex is not just about intercourse; it is about all kinds of body pleasuring. If we are talking about you at this point, you may care to explore those parts of Sexpieces 14, 15 and 16 that will contribute to your relationship.

Age is sometimes a cause for a man's loss of erection, but by no means as often as people allow themselves to imagine. Usually, as a man becomes older, the strength and frequency of his erections will begin to decline slowly. He is at the peak of his sexual potency in his late teens and thereafter he is imperceptibly diminishing in vigour. However, he can continue an active and potent sexual life well into old age, provided only that he believes in his own capacity and gives himself plenty of opportunities to exercise it. The trouble is that in our society there are so many cultural taboos against sex in middle and old age that we have actually come to believe that it does not happen, or that if it does, it is something rather perverse and disgusting. How could they! Children feel it about their parents and parents feel it about their own parents and this attitude, coupled with the view that a dirty old man is just acceptable but a dirty old woman certainly is not, means that many elderly people are quite literally brainwashed into thinking that sex is not for them, that they are too old for that sort of behaviour. If they accept this belief for too long, then they will find that it becomes a self-fulfilling prophecy. There is no doubt about it, you can get out of the habit of sex. This is all right, though sad if you never really got to like it, but definitely a pity if you did, and are only stopping because 'they' have decreed that it is not fitting for persons of advanced years. It may, however, sometimes become physically difficult for a woman whose vaginal tissue has become shrunken and thin after the menopause, because she will no longer lubricate easily, thus making intercourse painful. This can now often be remedied by a course of hormone replacement therapy, so if you are concerned about this, it is worth consulting a doctor.[7] In the case of a man there is a theory, backed by a considerable amount of evidence, that if a man does not use his erections regularly he may eventually lose them, for the same reason as with the woman, lack of practice. Age, therefore, may affect potency but only marginally, not drastically.

Boredom is another psychological reason we have not so far discussed but we strongly suspect that sheer tedium, a feeling of,

'I've done all this a million times before and I'm fed up' is behind much middle-aged impotence. Whose fault it is, is beside the point. If a couple who have been together for many years no longer find any joy or delight in their sex life, then they must decide for themselves whether they are going to try and revitalize it, in which case all the sexpieces up to number 17 are recommended to them. If, however, they decide just to leave it at that, then they must try to develop other aspects of their life together so that they can at least remain good companions. There is, of course, the third possibility, which is that they seek renewal with other partners. That is for them to decide, but may not be something that they can discuss frankly with one another or find an easy solution. Secretive extra-marital affairs are one problem; open marriage is another. It is fine in theory, but in practice it demands an immense amount of commitment, unselfishness and honesty from both people if it is to work.

Any man who has suffered the loss of erection even once in his life knows that far worse than the immediate feelings of shame and humiliation – especially if it happens with someone he cares about deeply – is the anxiety which follows. 'Is it going to happen again?' he asks himself, and finds that he is almost dreading the next occasion of intercourse. Fortunately, for most men it is just an occasional occurrence and if the afflicted man has an understanding partner she will help him through the crisis. Why impotence should affect some men and not others who may be subject to an equal amount of stress or psychological pressure is not clear, but it may be some men are most vulnerable in their sexual function, just as other people react to stress with diarrhoea or tension headaches.

For whatever reason, once impotence has begun to be a habit, a man will worry and worry and worry. The more he worries the worse it gets, and the worse it gets the more he worries, and that is bad news. His partner usually worries for him as well. At first she will try to hide her disappointment and then she tries to be kind by saying that it does not matter, which they both know to be untrue. Finally she ends by not being able to say or do anything right. If she pretends she has not noticed he may be temporarily relieved but he may accuse her, within himself, or openly to her face, of not caring enough about him and that it is because she is not trying to arouse him that he is impotent. If she notices, but tells him not to worry because she can wait and she is not worried and she understands, she has just told him three lies in succession and they both know that they are lies. Furthermore, they both know that these are no solutions and that his loss of erection does matter, to both of them, very much.

If you are in this situation and you have taken the precaution of checking with your doctor that there is no medical reason for your disability, then read the rest of this chapter very carefully.

Whatever your particular reason for losing your erection, the net effect of it is that a psychological cause has affected your physical responses. Even if it started off with a physical cause – too much alcohol for example – then the vicious circle that has been set up has a psychological centre to it. Just saying to yourself: 'I know what's wrong with me and I know it's ridiculous' is not a good enough instruction for your body. The aim of everything you have done so far is to persuade your body to resume its normal untroubled functioning by setting up those conditions which are most likely to establish effective sexual response. But, if you are reading this far, this may not have been enough.

A fear of abandoning themselves to their sexual feelings is the underlying cause of some men's impotence (see Case History 3). And the fear of it happening again is probably *the* single factor most likely to contribute to continuing impotence; another is the fear of being unable to meet the demands of their partner, whether she has expressed them or not. As you will have discovered through doing the sexpieces that you have completed, the first thing that a man suffering from these anxieties needs is to acquire the ability to please himself without worrying at all about whether he is able to please his partner. If he can unwind sufficiently to indulge himself sensually in some of the ways we have described in the first part of this book, and has learnt to accept his partner pleasuring him, without concentrating his attention on the presence or absence of an erection, then he has used these sexpieces properly.

When people are unhappy with themselves, it is not unusual for them to turn their anger and misery outwards on the person who is nearest to them. Thus a man may accuse his partner: it is her fault really because she is forever making impossible demands of him, not just in bed, but expecting him to earn more money, give her more help with the children and the household chores, spend more time listening to her grievances when does she not realize that he has had a long, hard day at the office? And so on and so forth. Similarly, a woman who is unsure of herself may be constantly demanding proofs of affection and commitment to her through his sexual performance: 'If you really loved me, you wouldn't be having this difficulty', or, 'I suppose you've got another woman because I'm getting old'. Often these accusations contain more than a half measure of truth, but when they become as sharp and bitter as this, then neither side is really thinking of the other any longer. They hurt themselves and each other.

Remember everything we have said about the importance of taking sexual responsibility for yourself. If you can both genuinely make a commitment to accepting that you and you alone are responsible for your body, but that for your relationship together to succeed you need each other's active involvement, then you are ready to start on the road back to recovery, rediscovering the pleasures of sex, and more about yourself as a person.

We have repeatedly stressed the need to create the right conditions for your love-making – privacy, plenty of time, freedom from other distractions, warmth and comfort. This time, why not try and take it all a bit further? Free your imagination. Shade the lights or substitute candles for them. Play your favourite music. Read each other passages from erotic books or share magazines with pictures that turn you on, and each other. Share some of your fantasies and, as you begin to relax, slip into Sexpiece 15, elaborating and developing it as you wish.

It is important that you give yourselves plenty of time for this stage because this type of pleasuring which has no goal beyond the immediate pleasure of being touched and stroked in all the most responsive parts of your body, enables you, the man, to relax and relieves the pressure to perform. Both of you give and ask for the pleasures that you have discovered together in all your previous sexpieces, and as you arouse one another, you (the man) will find that your erection begins to return. When this happens, you may both become so excited by its appearance and be so anxious 'not to waste it' that you will immediately try to have intercourse.

Resist this temptation! At this stage it really is the worst thing possible to do because the quicker you rush into using an erection the more probable it is that the difficulty will persist and then both of you will feel disappointed and let-down. It is like making a set of shelves and positioning them in the alcove to see how they look before finally securing them to the wall. If you put books on them at this stage they will inevitably collapse even though they look firm enough. Similarly with your returning erections; avoid using them until you are convinced that they are firmly established. And you will not be sure of this until you have done Sexpiece 18.

First, however, we want you to understand the purpose of this preliminary therapy using Sexpiece 15. It is to create a mood and a situation where a man can feel so relaxed and unanxious that his erections begin to come easily and frequently. The more this happens, the more confident you will both feel and the more regular and stronger his erections will become. Indeed, you will both find yourselves experiencing the reverse and positive side of what you have known hitherto. Just as anxiety feeds upon itself and looms larger with each disaster, so do confidence and self-esteem grow with each new and positive experience. Give yourselves time to enjoy this new power. Remember that an erection belongs to both of you and that you want to have time to enjoy it, to admire it and to play with it.

Now we want you to learn to accept that it is just as important to allow an erection to die away as it is to bring it to life, because the fear of not daring to let it go is the very thing which is likely to prevent it coming. Have you noticed that the word 'fear' has been introduced once again in a negative sense? Deliberately, because that is precisely the effect of an emotion like fear or anxiety. It is a killer of the things we desire most, so stop worrying, stop trying and just feel free to let your erections come and go.

From all that you have done already in the sexpieces, especially numbers 10 and 11, you will know that the feelings of pleasure and sexual arousal also come and go, depending on the amount of physical and psychological stimulation that you give each other or yourself. The more the touching and the mood are right, the stronger and more intense become your feelings of arousal and then, as you either diminish the intensity or lose interest, so your sense of arousal abates. This is absolutely the way it should be.

Sexpiece 18

Set up the situation of Sexpiece 10 and develop it along the following lines.

You, the man, lie on your back. Your partner begins massaging you all over your body, stroking and kneading and rubbing you in the ways she knows by now that you like best. You can direct her to do whatever you want and, gradually, the massage should travel up either from your legs or down from your shoulders and chest towards your penis and scrotum without, however, actually touching them. She begins to stroke the inside of your thighs or lets her fingers ripple down from your navel, along the hair line, dividing at the root of your penis where it joins your stomach, but not actually touching it. You will begin to find this no-touching touching increasingly exciting.

When his erection appears in response to this non-genital stimulation you, the woman, will extend your massage to the entire length of his penis, rubbing it with light, gentle strokes and using a cream which he likes. Bring the whole of your body, and yourself, to the art of pleasing him, perhaps kissing his penis or holding it between your breasts or doing anything else that you both enjoy. When he has had a firm erection for some minutes, deliberately let it die by reducing the stimulation.

This time, you, the woman, will take the limp penis in your hand and stroke it from base to tip with firm, slow, regular strokes. As you do this and it begins to swell and stiffen, he can encourage its growth by enjoying the sight of your body and losing himself in fantasies about what he would like to do with you. •

Whatever happens, do not go beyond this sexpiece to female superior intercourse (Sexpiece 19) until both of you feel confident that his erections are coming easily and frequently. If you, the woman, are becoming excited do not hide your feelings. If you want an orgasm, then Sexpiece 9 has taught you what you need to know and sharing a climax at this stage by masturbating yourself can only help your partner – if it should need any justification.

Sexpiece 19

You are now ready to use the man's erection for penetration. Stimulate the erection (woman) any way that you both enjoy and then, when it is firm and he is lying on his back, kneel over him with one leg on either side of his chest. Lower yourself on to the erect penis, reaching between your legs if necessary to place it at the vaginal entrance.

Since the woman is taking the responsibility for putting your penis inside herself, you (man) have nothing to fear and so can concentrate on the sensations you feel as her vagina slips over your penis. She wants it there, she has put it there; you have no obligations but to yourself and your own pleasure and in this undemanding situation you can start to be more active – touching, stroking and enjoying looking at your lover as she bends towards you. Both of you will be moving, she perhaps letting her vagina slide up and down your penis or using her vaginal muscles to grip and then relax her hold on it, while you will be concentrating on the sensations she is giving to your awakened penis. Gradually, you will take over more of the moving until you are ready to start thrusting, but she will continue moving with you so that you can both increase the stimulation as much as possible and pursue it to ejaculation when the moment seems inevitable and right.

It may well happen that things do not go quite as smoothly as this the very first time you try intercourse but, providing the man leaves the management of his erection to his lover and she accepts this responsibility, any apparent setbacks are experiences to learn from. If, for instance, his penis slips out of her vagina because it has gone limp she knows now how to stimulate it and this she can do and then put it back inside her. This may involve more than one try but they both know that he can have erections and they both want to enjoy them to climax; he trusts her ability to manage them. Armed with that degree of confidence there are no barriers. •

When you have had intercourse this way and feel happy about it, pick up the programme of sexual pleasuring at Sexpiece 15. Develop it by building on the experiences you have had in Sexpieces 18 and 19 and, most importantly, make sure that the woman feels free to ask for her arousal. Move on from 16 to 17.

Now the man is ready to take over the responsibility for his own erections and to use them whenever he wants to. Again he may find that every now and then he prefers his lover to take the responsibility while he lies there and is stimulated rather than taking the initiative himself. Far from being abnormal, this is absolutely natural. Every man wants to be passive sometimes and when he feels like this he should feel no embarrassment about indicating his wishes to his lover. If we had not all been so brainwashed by our cultural expectations to invest the male penis with superhuman qualities there would be fewer unhappy, impotent men and fewer frustrated women, miserably wondering if there is something wrong with them because they occasionally want to lead the action.

There is a less usual type of erectile insufficiency called anapriapism of which there was an example in Case History 4 where a man has no problems about getting an erection, but loses it at the moment of insertion. This is often connected with some profound anxiety or guilt, caused perhaps by an early childhood incident which the man himself may have completely forgotten. It may be that he dreads hurting his partner with his erect penis, which in some way he has come to associate with aggression or violence; or he may be unduly worried about her becoming pregnant, even when he knows that they are using a reliable contraceptive method; or he may be suffering from a deep dread of being hurt himself, the vagina-with-teeth syndrome.

Whatever the cause of this type of impotence, the treatment programme here will help, but special attention and time should be devoted to the transition from Sexpiece 18 to 19. It may be necessary for the woman to encourage him first to penetrate her vagina with his fingers in order to reassure himself that there is nothing harmful inside her – if that is his worry – or agree to use two types of contraceptive, a condom as well as the pill say, until she can persuade him to forget this fear. Above all, she must be confidently in charge of introducing his penis into her vagina.

11. She doesn't seem interested

The woman who does not 'turn on' has basically the same type of problem as the man who cannot get an erection. For a variety of reasons, some of which we shall examine more closely later in this chapter, she never or seldom feels aroused. This lack of response to what is happening to her in a potentially arousing situation manifests itself physically in an absence both of lubrication or engorgement of the vaginal tissue. Her nipples do not become erect nor does her skin colour change. However, unlike the man in a similar state who cannot, without an erection, have intercourse, a woman can, at a physical level, accept insertion, but it may well be painful; it will certainly be completely lacking in pleasure and generate deep feelings of being used.

We cannot stress too strongly how important the reaction of arousal is for enjoyable love-making, and especially intercourse. The man who insists on intercourse when there is no arousal in his partner is exactly equivalent to a woman who demands penetration when there is no erection.

Frigid is the old way of describing an unaroused woman. It suggests someone cold, aloof and uncaring, possibly hostile to men, whereas in reality many women who find that they are unable to respond to the sexual advances of their partner mind desperately and, almost invariably, they will blame themselves for their so-called inadequacy. It also does not make a clear distinction between the two types of sexual dysfunction (an ugly word, but we use it here to avoid the pejorative sense of frigid) women may suffer from and, even now, is not completely understood, despite the work of Masters and Johnson. Some women may become easily aroused, yet frequently or occasionally fail to have an orgasm.

This chapter is devoted to the problems of the unaroused

woman while in the following one we concentrate on those of the non-orgasmic woman, but obviously both conditions can be, and often are, present in the same person.

What does cause this condition? Even the most sexually responsive women fluctuate in the amount of libido (desire) they feel, and this is also true for men. Many women find that they are less interested in sex in the middle of their monthly cycle when the hormones of oestrogen and progesterone are at their peak. This could be Nature's way of effecting contraception as this is also the time of month when they are most likely to be ovulating. Drugs and tranquillizers, especially if they are taken habitually, may have a lowering effect on sexual responsiveness as will depression, excessive stress and worry, and sheer physical fatigue. However, the vast majority of women who are suffering from a lack of interest in sex and, more specifically, a failure to respond to stimulation, do so either because they are not being stimulated effectively or because they fear abandoning themselves to their sexual feelings.

Let us start with the problem of inadequate stimulation. This could be due to something as simple, and as easy to put right, as ignorance. The man may be too hurried, too eager to start thrusting and so bring himself to orgasm, without being aware of his partner's pattern of response. For instance, she may not like being touched genitally, immediately. She may prefer to be kissed and caressed and soothed into a state of warm relaxed expectation. She may like her breasts being fondled but he never does this, or alternatively, she may find that the way he touches her is too hard and too insistent. She may not know where her clitoris is, but expect her partner to know, as if by divine inspiration, exactly what pleases her, and where and how much. Generally speaking, women are more variable and subtle in their sexual responses, but it is hardly fair to expect a man to understand her individual desires if she is reluctant to confide them to him. It may be that she is afraid to tell him because it will make him angry with her – he will assume that she is casting aspersions on his prowess as a lover – or because she fears that he will reject her.

Many women who claim that they have never been aroused in

their lives may have forgotten their early sexual experiences when they indulged in quite heavy petting sessions during which they became very responsive and excited. They would have felt wetness between their legs and a feeling of urgent pressure, almost pain, as the blood flowed into their genitals, but because they did not 'go all the way' and perhaps also because they had never been told to expect these sensations and to regard them as quite normal, they may have put them out of their mind. This is especially probable in cases where a girl has been brought up to think of pre-marital intercourse as sinful or socially undesirable or cheapening.

Although religious influences are less powerful today, their effects still linger on. We impose a dual standard of behaviour on young people, disapproving of the girl who 'sleeps around' but smiling benignly on the young man who is 'sowing his wild oats' and supposedly gaining experience for the time when he wants to settle down and get married. In fact, it often happens that his experience, even if fairly wide, is not particularly profound because he has been using women rather than sharing in the discovery of their sexuality.

Fear of pregnancy is another worry for many people. Although it is now widely known that the pill and other forms of contraception are freely available, a young woman is sometimes shy to ask her doctor or admit to her friends that she does not know where to go to obtain supplies. Much more significantly, many girls do not want to make the commitment of going on the pill because, deep down, they are not ready to commit themselves to sexual intercourse. This means that either they indulge in unconsummated heavy petting or they are eventually persuaded into intercourse, but because they are so frightened of the possible consequences, they do not really enjoy it, and of course they risk pregnancy.

We are sometimes tempted to think that because our technological knowledge has increased by leaps and bounds, therefore our emotions and attitudes have also kept pace with the changes. Human beings do adapt surprisingly well to quite drastic changes in their environment but they are always much slower to revise their beliefs and reasons for action in the light of new knowledge, however convincingly presented. Let us also remember that even if children no longer learn their prayers at their mother's knees, they certainly acquire her prejudices and absorb her attitudes about sex from a tender age.

Closely linked to the sex-is-sin view is the idea that sex-is-dirty, except for the purpose of procreating children. Although we hope that by now we have convinced you that the only wrong thing about sex is when it *feels* bad or unsatisfying because it has not been pleasurable, it remains a sad fact that many people are still growing up with the idea that there is something a bit disgusting about letting yourself go in sex. Such behaviour reminds them too much of the animal side of their nature. Well, of course, we are animals with what sometimes seems to be the dubious advantage of having an exceptionally well-developed brain which acts as a controller as well as an instructor and a communicator of messages. If a girl has been made to feel guilty about her body throughout childhood and adolescence, made to feel that what goes on below her navel is something to be ashamed of rather than proud, encouraged to conceal her menstruation, to ignore her erotic emotions, to romanticize rather than sexualize her youthful affections, she may eventually take refuge from all the fears those prohibitions produce in her by shrinking from any touch that might produce the forbidden sensation of sexual pleasure. Plainly, if she then brings these inhibitions into her marriage, where the essence of the relationship is intimacy expressed through touching, both she and her husband face serious problems.

These are some of the moral attitudes which may affect a woman's capacity to experience sexual arousal. There are also the broader cultural expectations of how a woman should behave in relation to men which, to some extent, we have already touched on in earlier chapters. Most girls are still brought up to see themselves always in a position of dependency; in order to ensure that that state of servitude is bearable they learn to please, to serve and to live through others. In sex this means that they defer to the man's supposedly superior knowledge and more urgent sexual needs. If this means that they derive no pleasure from sex because they would not presume to ask for anything for themselves for fear of appearing aggressive, selfish or critical, then so be it. This attitude explains why some women appear able to endure a lifetime of unsatisfactory sex with apparent equanimity, unlike a man in the same situation who, precisely because he has been indoctrinated with the equally crippling injunction that he must always perform and perform successfully, is invariably unmanned by any 'failure'. As Helen Kaplan[5] puts it so well: 'Our society fosters female dependency and male exploitation: guilt in girls about achievement and guilt in boys about failure to achieve. These role assignments are exceedingly harmful to *both* genders, not only in the area of sexual functioning but in other areas of life as well.'

Some women are better able than others to resist the pressures and restrictions which have been imposed on them in childhood and adolescence and will emerge as unscathed and healthily functioning sexual beings. Why some women, like some men, are more vulnerable to stress, and reflect this vulnerability in their sexual life, remains a mystery.

There are other personal reasons which may cause a woman to lose interest in sex, perhaps only temporarily, or after a long period of being normally responsive and orgasmic. It may be that the quality of her relationship with her lover has deteriorated. Just as a man who is bored with his partner can become impotent with her, so a woman may equally become bored and unaroused by a man who always makes love in the same unimaginative way. She may not love him or even like him very much any more.

Sometimes, at the beginning of a relationship, a woman may have had no problems about becoming sexually aroused, but because the man persistently fails to satisfy her and she is continually left feeling physically uncomfortable and emotionally deeply disappointed, she finally reacts by blocking off altogether. She cannot bear to experience any more let-downs, but unfortunately for both of them, neither can she summon up her courage to talk the matter out openly and completely. A relationship left to fester in this way for too long with unspoken hostilities mounting between the couple may become very difficult to restore, unless both of them can develop an understanding of the importance of helping each other to become self-responsible individuals which, in this context, specifically means that she may ask and he will agree that she can be 'selfish' about her erotic needs.

Before explaining how this may be done through our self-help programme, there are just two other possible causes for a woman's failure to feel sexual arousal which should be briefly mentioned. We referred earlier to fatigue. Many women exhaust themselves by packing too much into their daily life. They may be combining a job with running a home and bringing up a young family; or they may be imbued with a 'Superwoman' complex which makes it incumbent on them to achieve everything unaided, the 'where would they be without me?' attitude. Much has been said about a similar drive among men to prove how indispensable they are, resulting too often in a coronary thrombosis or early death after retirement, but the less dramatic manifestation among women should not be ignored. A woman who can hardly get herself to bed because she is so drained of energy can, quite truthfully, say, 'Not tonight, darling. I'm too tired.' But if it happens too often, and she does care about her sexual relationship and is not using fatigue as an excuse to turn away unwelcome attentions, then she and her partner should seriously re-examine their way of life and see whether they cannot share out more of the domestic burdens and in other ways reduce the demands on her.

Finally, there is the not unusual phenomenon of the woman who finds that she has become less interested in sex after the birth of a child. Again there may be purely physical reasons behind this; the demands of feeding and coping with endlessly interrupted nights are exhausting. If it is a first child, she may be overanxious and defensive about her capacity as a mother; and some husbands, usually rather immature men, may resent her concern with the baby and jealously demand more of her attention, rather than attempt to help her get over the first difficult weeks. Physically, she will be at a low ebb anyway, after the effort of childbirth, and there is the additional hazard of post-natal depression which varies in intensity but affects many more women than we like to believe. It is also possible that she finds intercourse painful as a result of clumsy stitching of her perineum and birth canal immediately after birth. If you suspect this to be your problem or that you could be suffering from post-natal depression, then it is essential to visit your doctor. There are other conflicts arising out of the birth of a child which may cause blocked sexual responses and require more skilled therapeutic attention if they persist, but most couples find that they do eventually emerge relatively unharmed from a testing time, although they would have found it easier to cope with if they had been given some advance warning of what to expect.

It may surprise you to realize that there are so many possible causes for lack of arousal and that so few of them are the result of a directly physical malfunction, but we believe it is important that men, as well as women, should realize how extremely vulnerable a woman is to the many and varied strains and pressures which crowd in on her and sometimes prevent her from being the person she could be. There are, of course, the exceptional cases where a woman has never in her life experienced arousal, just as there are the rare men who have never had an erection, due usually (in both sexes) to traumatizing experiences in childhood or adolescence, but we do not think that there are very many genuinely unresponsive women.

As with the treatment we described in the last chapter, the purpose here is to create a warm, relaxed sensuous atmosphere in which the man devotes his loving, undemanding and undivided attention to the needs of his lover. If, hitherto, she has always left it to him to take the initiatives and please her the way he thinks fit, they may both find it difficult at first to reverse roles, but all the work up to Sexpiece 14 has been directed towards encouraging this flexibility.

During the sexpieces up to number 11 we would expect the woman to have been experiencing the early stages of arousal: wetness around the vaginal opening from the lubricant and some, if not all, of the other physical reactions that we describe in *Let's Look Again*, the chapter about sexual arousal. Some women who are now reading this chapter may have found Sexpiece 9 quite difficult to do. If you experienced no difficulty, then move straight on to the next sexpiece. If you did find Sexpiece 9 rather difficult but during Sexpieces 4 to 8 you felt warm, relaxed, receptive and enjoyed your bodily sensations, and during number 11 found the same feelings developing more strongly, then you too might care to move on to the next sexpiece. It may do the unblocking for you and certainly no harm will come from the experience. However, do not work too hard to produce arousal because that could become counter-productive and may indicate that you need the help of a skilled therapist to unravel the reasons behind the blocking.

Sexpiece 20

Refer back to Sexpiece 11 and, as a development of that, set up the following situation.

The man sits up against the back of the bed, his own back propped by pillows and his legs wide apart. The woman sits between his legs, leaning back against his chest. Make sure that you both feel comfortable and relaxed, and that your weight is well supported. It is not very easy to talk in this tandem position but it is an ideal way for the woman to take her man's hand and teach him to touch her caressingly and teasingly over all the most sensitive parts of her body.

Teach him how to play with your breasts and circle your nipples. Let him stroke your stomach and show him how to edge down towards your mons pubis (the bony mound above your clitoris and vagina) and teach him how to pleasure you. This is where the value of knowing how to masturbate is evident. If you know how to excite yourself it becomes much easier to tell your lover what to do, but do not worry if you still feel a bit shy about masturbating. Just accept that it may take longer to become aroused if you are learning through someone else's fingers.

If this position becomes uncomfortable or you want a change, let the woman lie on her back and ask the man to caress her any way she wants. Use a body lotion if you would like this session to continue for some time and there is a likelihood of the man's continued massaging causing painful friction, but remember that it makes no more sense to apply lotion or KY jelly if the vagina has not already become naturally wet than it would be to tie a splint on a limp penis.

The woman's task is to stay inside her skin and enjoy the sensations she is generating and receiving. The very early sexpieces of bathing and listening to each other's bodies were part of this process of unblocking the channels of sensation. Her sensations, particularly in the lower part of her pelvis, are the best guide as to how the sexpiece is progressing and, just as for the man, her feelings of arousal will vary according to the intensity of physical and mood stimulation she is receiving. •

Enjoy being aroused and when you are, you can take this sexpiece on to Sexpiece 15, or intercourse, as you prefer. But if you choose intercourse it must be because you want it, not just because you want to please your man.

Sexpiece 21

If the man has not already got an erection, stimulate one. Either of you can do this, but he should be lying on his back so that she can lower herself on to his erect penis, kneeling with one leg on either side of him.

Contain his penis and concentrate on the sensations you are feeling inside your vagina. Squeeze your vaginal muscles. Explore the length of his penis by sliding gently up and down it. Explore the sensation of your clitoris, either by rubbing against your man or using your or his fingers to stimulate you. If he feels he wants to climax and you are not ready, you should disengage for a few minutes but he should continue stimulating you with his fingers.

Remember it is you, the woman, who is being treated, so both must concentrate on producing your pleasure. But the more aroused you become, the more excited he will feel which, in turn, will help you to intensify your excitement. You may want to change from your female superior position (kneeling over him) to lying side by side or on your back. Do whatever you want but always continue to concentrate on your vaginal sensations.

Now you know what it feels like to be aroused, having an orgasm will come from following your feelings, intensifying them, giving in to them and letting them carry you off. You may enjoy Sexpiece 16 as a way of exploring this and taking it on to 17 or you may prefer to try out the ideas in Sexpiece 22 in the next chapter. •

It sometimes happens that a man experiences an unaccustomed rapid arousal because of his partner's new interest and this may cause him to ejaculate prematurely. Once or twice does not matter, so long as the love-making does not end there, but if it starts to become habitual, then it might be advisable to learn the squeeze technique (see Chapter 13, *He Comes Too Soon*).

Another occasional side effect is that the woman so enjoys her new sensations of arousal that the man may begin to worry about his capacity to meet her demands, even to the extent of experiencing a brief period of loss of erection. If this should happen, then go back to Sexpieces 10 and 15, remembering how important it is to be leisurely, to please yourself and not to set any goals in your love-making, apart from taking full advantage of the pleasure of being involved with someone else's body. After all, the whole purpose of treating yourself to sex is to enjoy yourself. It makes no sense to remove one hang-up only to find that another has taken its place. But if you have both followed the earlier part of the treatment in the way we suggested, you should both by now have enough confidence in yourselves and each other to overcome any temporary setbacks.

12. She never comes

More has been written and said, speculated and surmised, guessed and dogmatized about the female orgasm than almost any other aspect of sexual behaviour. It has been described and analysed, measured and labelled, alternately ignored and hailed as man's greatest gift to woman. Some women have spent their whole lives faking it and other women spend their time worrying, either because they think they are not getting enough orgasms or they fear they are not having the right kind. Some women are desperate because they have never had an orgasm and other women are desperate about what would happen to them if they did. They fear they might explode or die or never recover from the shame of having let themselves go in front of someone else.

The whole subject has become riddled with myth and mis-understanding, and for too many women it has become a cause for misery instead of being a natural source of exquisite bodily and emotional pleasure. So what are the facts? Let us ask a few questions and see what answers we get, bearing in mind that even the experts admit that they do not yet know everything.

Is orgasm every time, preferably multiple, indispensable to a woman's sexual satisfaction? No. Many women derive great pleasure from the total sexual contact, the fondling, caressing, kissing and general display of erotic affection given to them by a sensitive lover which may not always culminate in a climax. (The same is true for men.) However, they would begin to feel dis-satisfied if, time after time, they did not have an orgasm and this situation would worsen if they started to worry about it, in the same way as the man who worried about getting an erection finds that his anxiety about 'next time' makes him even less capable of functioning.

What is an orgasm? Basically it is a series of rhythmic reflex contractions of the muscles of the pelvic floor which are experienced as a pulsing sensation in the entrance area of the vaginal canal. It is triggered by stimulating sexually sensitive parts of the body, of which the clitoris and the breasts are the most important. Some women experience orgasm by having their breasts and nipples alone touched in the right way, or by being stimulated on other parts of their body, round the vaginal entrance, for instance, or the back passage. A few women, who are exceptionally easily aroused to orgasm, may be stimulated by touch on even more distant erogenous zones – behind the ears, for example – or by having an erotic dream or fantasy.

The experience of orgasm differs from woman to woman and from occasion to occasion. Some experience it as a high peak of pleasure which fades away rapidly. Others come to the peak and then feel it rippling on and on for seconds and even minutes, maintaining them on a high plateau of pleasure. Others feel it as a more internal, diffuse, warm sensation spreading throughout the lower part of their body. It may be helpful to think of orgasm as being rather like the high jump where the bar can be made higher and lower, but the lower the bar the easier it is to go over the top. Obvious things which make the bar lower are being in good health, making love with someone you really like, feeling warm and relaxed and uninhibited, being in the right mood, not being distracted by the kids or feeling worried about anything. Technically, this bar is called the threshold and there is no doubt that some women, whatever their circumstances or psychological background, have it fixed much lower than others. Most women, however are vulnerable to some degree to adverse surroundings or influences, and very often a woman who has found herself to be non-orgasmic on one occasion for perhaps some minor reason, may then find herself caught in a revolving wheel of arousal carried forward to the peak of pleasure and ... dropped away from it at the very last moment. This may happen because she is frightened of a repeat disappointment and so decides to hold herself back, or perhaps because her lover has stopped stimulating her in order to get himself into a better position just as she was about to come. Many men do not realize that a woman needs continuous stimulation for orgasm.

Do women have more than one sort of orgasm? This hoary old debate has been going on ever since Freud first suggested that there were two types of female orgasm – the clitoral and the vaginal. Not content with creating what we now know, mainly as the result of clinical research by Masters and Johnson, to be a false dichotomy, he and his psychoanalytical followers proceeded also to create two kinds of woman to fit the two types of orgasm.

The woman who only achieves climax through clitoral stimulation is, they said, sexually infantile to the point of neurosis because she has never progressed beyond her early erotic experimentation, whereas the woman who, while enjoying clitoral sensation experiences orgasm vaginally when she is filled by a strong, hard penis, is mature and fully adapted to her female sexuality. It is not hard to see why this argument should have caused bitter and protracted controversy. It is doubtful if anyone cares too much about hurt feelings among the sexperts, but the damage caused to the psyche and lives of countless thousands of women who have been led to believe by doctors and misleading articles that they are frigid and inadequate if they do not have marvellous vaginal orgasms, every time, is incalculable.

Recently, a new and, in our view, no less potentially harmful dimension has been introduced to the argument. Certain voices in the women's movement have declared that the only sort of orgasm experienced by women is clitoral, in other words, orgasm which does not depend on penile stimulation. Therefore, they conclude, to insist on the 'myth' of the vaginal orgasm, implying that a woman can only achieve sexual satisfaction through full intercourse with a man, is the most blatant example of male chauvinism. To some extent, but not entirely, they are supported by the physiological facts. As we saw in the chapter *Let's Look Again*, the vagina is not a particularly sensitive part of the body, having few or no nerve endings except around the entrance and just inside. We also know that, without effective clitoral stimulation, a woman is unlikely to be sufficiently aroused to have an orgasm. (Later in this chapter, when we suggest some of the ways in which a woman can treat herself to orgasm, many of them involve continuous clitoral stimulation throughout intercourse.) However, although the clitoris is almost always essential to a woman's orgasm, its function is as a source of sensation triggering the muscular reflex of orgasm which is then experienced in the vaginal area, not just in the clitoris. In other words, orgasm includes both clitoral and vaginal elements and, in some cases, it may include the experience of contractions of the womb as well.

You may well be wondering what all the fuss is about. Either a woman has orgasms, or she does not. If she does, there is no problem and if she does not? Yes, there is a problem but surely one which is no more nor less insoluble than the other sex difficulties for which sex therapy is now trying to provide some of the answers. Unfortunately, it is not as simple as that. For one thing, women often find it very hard to describe what they experience in orgasm, partly because, as we explained in our answer to the second question, *What is an orgasm?*, there are subtle variations in the degree and intensity of orgasm experienced by one and the same woman on different occasions and between individual women. For another, women have been indoctrinated not to talk about their sexual feelings, indeed not to think of themselves as sexual beings. Feminine certainly, but that is symbolized in a pretty face, curvaceous figure and winning ways, not by displaying a frank interest in their own sexuality.

It is for these reasons that although so much has been said about what women should feel in orgasm, and so much distress and anxiety instilled in those who suspect that they do not measure up to the norm, whatever that may be as laid down by male experts, until very recently nobody has paid much attention to the feelings and opinions of women themselves. Things are changing, however. The combination of the growing strength and demands coming from the women's movement, together with the first ever properly conducted scientific research into human sexual behaviour (Masters and Johnson) has meant that women are becoming much more courageous about declaring openly what they feel. Sexual liberation is integral to the whole liberation movement and this involves simply not accepting any longer what other people say a woman should think and feel in her sexual life until she has tested the water herself.

The best guide to deciding whether or not you have had an orgasm is whether you feel satisfied. Arousal which does not lead to a climax of any kind will leave you with a feeling of frustration which can range from vague dissatisfaction to intense physical and mood discomfort. (For some good accounts of what it feels like to be a sexual woman read *Our Bodies Ourselves*[8] and *The Hite Report*[4].)

Is it important for a man and a woman making love to have simultaneous orgasm? No. Sometimes it does happen and when it does, it can be an exceptionally moving experience, but more often it does not and it really is not important provided that both partners are satisfied by their love-making and are orgasmic at the moment when they are ready for it. Clearly, the man who consistently ejaculates during intercourse long before his partner has been aroused to the point of climax is depriving her of her satisfaction. Sex between any two people is unique and good sex lies in knowing how to make it work reliably in that unique situation.

What makes a woman have an orgasm? Effective stimulation and an uninhibited enjoyment of her sexual pleasure, whether she is alone or with her lover. If she is with her lover, then she will also want to feel total confidence in him and delight in his love-making.

What stops a woman having an orgasm? Lack of the above, but there are other possible factors too. Some women have never had an orgasm in their life. This may be due to lack of experience, unexplored fears, an insufficiently skilled partner, no knowledge of how to masturbate or simply ignorance.

We mentioned earlier the fear many women have of abandoning themselves to sensations which they feel are too powerful for them, rather like standing on a high diving board and feeling too frightened to jump, so they never climb up there at all. Others are worried about what they will look like to their partner if they let themselves go – undignified perhaps, noisy and uncontrolled. Men, too, suffer from this fear, both on their own and their partner's behalf. Often these are people who have been brought up in a somewhat restricted, inhibited family where it was considered bad form to show too much feeling, especially anger or unrestrained enthusiasm.

Sometimes it is the circumstances of people's lives which cause the trouble. For instance, the young couple who have to start married life in one room in the home of one or other of their parents are naturally going to feel very inhibited about their sex life, especially if sex has been a taboo subject. Not only are they cramped and on top of others who can no doubt hear most of what goes on behind thin walls, but those others are not like the ordinary anonymous inmates of a bed-sitting house; they are parents, people who, until recently, have been exercising control over them and, even now, may find it difficult to relinquish authoritarian attitudes. That could be bad enough in the everyday transactions of life, but when it also infringes on the sexual privacy of their adult children, then it may well prove disastrous. Even when there are not these off-putting conditions and the couple indeed have as much privacy and uninterrupted time as they need, they may find that it is this very atmosphere of exclusive, one-to-one intimacy which they find daunting and burdensome. Many women who feel like this are capable of masturbating themselves easily to orgasm – on their own – but cannot relax enough to involve their partner.

Another problem many women have with orgasm is that they remain too conscious of themselves throughout sexual activity, not in the right 'selfish' way which, as we have seen in earlier chapters, is essential for complete sexual satisfaction, but as an outsider constantly watching their own performance. The thoughts that run through their head include: *What does he think of me? Does he really like me? Am I doing this badly? Am I too slow and making him impatient?* Unfortunately, the more you think about anything to do with sex in a goal-orientated way, the less likely you are to achieve the success you are seeking.

A woman who catches herself doing this and finds herself being constantly frustrated because she is not getting orgasms, should also ask herself why she is so anxious. Maybe she fears losing her lover, or being rejected by him, and this anxiety has caused her to block sexually. Or is she afraid of asking him to please her in ways which she fears he will find threatening? It is very important that women who do find themselves inhibited by fears of this nature should try to talk out their problems with the person who can help them best and matters to them most – their lover.

There are some women who, no matter what sex therapy is applied, seem incapable of ever having an orgasm. Nobody quite knows why this should be so, but an educated guess is that it may be that the psychological condition which caused the inhibition in the first place has become so deeply entrenched that it has actually destroyed the woman's capacity to function orgasmically. Such a rare situation should not be confused with the far more frequent case where a woman, after years of frustration because she cannot seem to achieve orgasm, decides to adapt herself to accepting what is apparently an inalterable physiological fact. Often such a woman will say something like, 'I don't mind for myself, but I wish I could for X's sake', as if it were entirely her fault or, alternatively, she will play the game of faking orgasms, time after time and year after year, 'just to keep him happy', with the result that she herself becomes progressively less and less interested in sex. Hardly surprising since, by setting her mind against the possibility of finding anything pleasurable in sex, she makes it increasingly likely that she never will get anything out of it.

Equally destructive to the prospect of pleasure is the attitude of mind which puts the blame entirely on the other person. In some cases, where there is profound sexual ignorance, this may be largely true, but usually the sexual fears and ignorance are shared by both partners and anyway, fault is something we should avoid attributing in a sexual relationship. Remember what we have said about the importance of assuming responsibility for one's own sexual life and do not build up a barricade of blame and hostility towards the other person. This will only have the effect of utterly destroying your sexual communication, and reinforcing the blame.

It is for this reason that we start with masturbation as a treatment for helping the non-orgasmic woman. Since the problem is often rooted in the woman's fear of letting herself go, it is usually better for her to begin by treating herself, allowing herself to enjoy the pleasure of orgasm, on her own, undisturbed, and without any fears of what her lover may say or think, or how he may look at her.

Look again at Sexpiece 9 and if you want some more ideas we suggest that you read Betty Dodson's book called *Liberating Masturbation*[6] and *The Hite Report*,[4] both of which carry detailed descriptions of the different ways women can masturbate. Do not worry if you did not get very far into masturbation in your work-through to Sexpiece 14. Sexpieces 10 to 14 will have helped in the loosening-up process and you may well find masturbation easier now that you return to it. Think about using a vibrator. These can be bought by mail order[9] or from sex shops and provide much more intense, rapid stimulation than anything you can do with your fingers. However, some women do not like them because they seem mechanical, which they are, and sometimes they do not work for the individual woman. If this happens to you, do not be disappointed but try something else.

It may be that you are too self-conscious and anxious about yourself, or it may be that you are frightened of having an orgasm for one or other of the reasons that we discussed earlier. If this is the case then what you need is distraction, and the ideal way to distract yourself is by doing something which stimulates you into desiring more and more pleasure. Try indulging in your favourite erotic fantasy and, if you are not aware of having any, then read about other people's in a book like Nancy Friday's *My Secret Garden*[10] or anything else which you find erotic. At the same time, masturbate yourself, using your fingers, your vibrator or anything else that turns you on. Make sure that you are warm and in a comfortable position. Play a favourite record ... and relax.

Once you have found ways of bringing yourself to orgasm, and you will find it easier than perhaps you imagine possible, using one or all of these methods, then the time has come to involve your lover. Now you know how to stimulate your clitoris, you want to apply this skill to intercourse.

Some women find that, although they are easily aroused and come easily if their clitoris is sufficiently stimulated, they cannot get an orgasm through intercourse. Do remember, though, that you don't have to have an orgasm through intercourse. We have stressed all along that there are many ways of being orgasmic. Intercourse is just one of them. What is right for you is what works for you, so try and get away from the idea that you ought to have an orgasm through intercourse. If you do want this experience then experiment with positions which maintain a high level of clitoral stimulation throughout intercourse.

Sexpiece 22

One way of doing this is by making love in a position where the woman continues to feel pressure on her clitoris while the man is thrusting.

You, the woman, kneel over him in the female superior position and as you both move together, you can control the pressure of your clitoris against the pubic bone. A development of this technique is that he stimulates your clitoris with his fingers at the same time as he is thrusting with his penis, either in this position or when you are lying side by side. As you become more practised at doing this, he can withhold the clitoral stimulation for short periods to start with, gradually lengthening them until finally you are sufficiently aroused by the movement of his penis inside you not to need the clitoral stimulation any more. However, he should be ready to resume it at once if you signal that your arousal peak is slackening off, because it is very important that there should be no break in stimulation of some kind, although the quality and intensity of it may be as varied as you want.

Another way of bringing yourself to orgasm, and one that your lover will also find very arousing, is for you to masturbate yourself when his penis is inside you. You can then bring yourself almost to the point of climax at which moment he takes over and completes it by thrusting and bringing himself to climax, carrying you with him.

If a woman is to have an orgasm during intercourse, it is absolutely essential that she be highly aroused *before* the man enters her with his penis. Although this may seem fairly obvious, in fact it often happens that a man wrongly assumes that because a woman is lubricating and reacting responsively she is, therefore, ready for him. Naturally, she should not be leaving all the initiatives to him, so the better she understands her own body the better able she will be to indicate when she wants to be filled by his penis. The woman who is aware of her vaginal sensations will know that the pleasure of holding a slow-moving, deeply-thrusting penis within her is quite different from the sensations she gets when her clitoris is stimulated. One is not better than the other but they are distinguishable, both in the pleasure they produce and the sensation.

At this stage in the sexpiece and whichever method you are trying, you, the woman, should concentrate entirely on your own sensations and forget completely any ideas you may have had (usually false anyway) about appearing to be demanding or that your lover will become tired of stimulating you. Use your vaginal muscles and feel them pressing against the penis. The more you can develop this vaginal awareness, the more likely it will be that eventually you will be able to come during intercourse. •

These are different suggestions for different occasions. Try out what appeals to you and do not feel let down if one or other does not work for you. The most essential thing for any woman who wants to have orgasm, either for the first time in her life or to recover a lost potential, is to take it easy. Orgasm is a pleasure, not a task, so give yourself up to it and let it take you where it will.

13. He comes too soon

We have already briefly described in *What makes sex go wrong and how do we know?* the easily recognized pattern of premature ejaculation; Case History 9 is a typical example of how this lack of voluntary control over ejaculation can cause serious concern in a sexual relationship. More difficult to determine is why it should happen to certain men and not to others. The origins of it as a problem are varied.

It may stem from the early, hurried sexual encounters so many young men have, say on the back seat of a car or in the girl's home, when they are plagued by the fear of being discovered with the result that his over-riding concern is to climax as rapidly as possible. It may reflect a man's anxiety about his performance or an obscure, unresolved conflict about his attitude to women generally, possibly a subconscious dislike or fear which he vents by satisfying himself without caring for his partner's feelings. More generally, however, it is now regarded as a lack of voluntary control of the reflex mechanism of ejaculation and it is from this standpoint that treatment is likely to be most beneficial.

It is certain that, whatever the causes, the effects of persistent premature ejaculation can be very destructive to a relationship. A situation builds up where the man feels increasingly anxious and nervous each time he approaches intercourse and these are the very emotions most likely to trigger off the too-early response. Meanwhile the woman, who is persistently denied her opportunity to experience complete arousal and, therefore, orgasm during intercourse, will come to feel exceedingly used by her partner. An experienced and sympathetic woman may be prepared to tolerate this for a while and indeed strive to help her lover to delay by any means that she can think of, but over an extended period she too will be frustrated and resentful at being abandoned in the early stages of arousal.

A few couples cope with the problem by the man giving the woman manual clitoral stimulation to orgasm after he has ejaculated, but in the circumstances of premature ejaculation this feels like a substitute for genuine climax rather than a valid experience among the many varieties of climax possible. Usually what happens is that both turn off sex with each other: he, because he dare not face what he feels is inevitable failure; and she, because she can no longer bear the disappointment, with the result that from one problem, another arises – her gradual loss of arousal. Their repressed anger and tensions mount, creating yet another vicious cycle which, if it is not broken by frank discussion and learning how to establish control, may sour the relationship beyond redemption.

Ironically, although it is well known that premature ejaculation is one of the most common male sexual problems it is not nearly so well appreciated that it is also the easiest to cure. The penis is a sensitive trigger to ejaculation and the aim of the self-help treatment we shall describe in this chapter is to retain the pleasures of its sensitivity while removing the consequences of its reacting too swiftly to stimulation. Quite simply, it is a matter of learning a straightforward technique and we will take you through it, step by step. If you follow our instructions carefully and give yourselves enough time – three weeks is the minimum period in which you can expect to establish control – the problem should be overcome.

Let us remind you that we are addressing ourselves to you as a couple. This is because, although the man always feels it to be his problem and one which it is up to him to solve, in fact it is a problem which is shared by the woman because – and we cannot repeat this enough either – a good, strong and reliable erection belongs as much to her as to her lover, and it is for both of them to enjoy.

It might look at this point as if we are becoming involved in performance routines, yet we know that nothing is more damaging to enjoyable sex than concentrating so intensely on performance that pleasure is blocked. We hold no brief for performance-orientated sex. However, when sex is not working well, it is necessary to look in detail at what is causing the disruption in order to remove these mechanical blocks which are hindering spontaneous enjoyment. Knowing that his performance is unsatisfactory has the disastrous effect of making a man concentrate ever more intensely on his actions but less and less on his *reactions*, in other words on his own feelings and sensations which are leading him to climax.

Quite a mythology has grown up about the desperate measures many men resort to in order to control ejaculation. Convinced that their problem lies in being too swiftly aroused and unaware that they can control their reflexes, they try to force control of their sensations by switching off sexually as soon as they feel the mounting excitement threatening to overwhelm them. They will adopt all manner of stratagems to take their minds off what is about to happen, like imagining disasters or remembering the names of stations on the Northern Line. Inevitably their distraction communicates itself to their partner and, since she is unlikely to have been told why he is behaving like this, all she is aware of is that he seems suddenly to have lost interest in her. Even if he has told her that he is trying to control his ejaculation she invariably becomes concerned on his behalf and this inhibits her own arousal, thus making the demand on him to hold back from climax even stronger. Eventually her disturbance and disappointment may rebound on him to the extent that instead of merely restraining himself, he finds that he has lost his erection.

Couples who have been through this experience, or variations of it, do not need to be told how distressing it can be, particularly if it becomes habitual. Notice that in the reactions we have described above, the man typically tries to control the level of sensation and it is this which leads to the cycle of decline.

The technique we are about to describe depends upon appreciating the sensations in the build-up to ejaculation and so becoming aware how to control the underlying reflex. It is a combination of the Seman stop-start method, named after a doctor of that name who taught it to his patients in the fifties and the more recent Masters and Johnson 'squeeze' method which is an elaboration of the same basic idea.

You will have already worked through to Sexpiece 14. Now your first aim is to learn to place control of the man's ejaculatory process with the woman.

Sexpiece 23

Both of you are naked. The man lies on his back and the woman kneels between his legs and starts to stimulate an erection.

You, the woman, use the hand you use ordinarily for everyday tasks like writing or opening a door, namely the hand with the stronger grasp. Have some body lotion or KY jelly available in order to avoid causing painful friction. When his penis is vertical in front of you with the underside facing you, place your thumb on the point where the glans meets the main shaft of the penis. This you will remember is called the frenulum and it is the most sensitive area of the penis. Keeping your thumb in position, place your first finger directly behind the thumb and just above the coronal ridge while the second finger is also opposite the thumb but just below the coronal ridge.

Now you are ready to apply the squeeze technique.

Continue to arouse him by caressing and rubbing his penis, but as soon as he becomes aware of being on the edge of climax he must tell you or motion to you with some signal that you both understand. Immediately your fingers grasp the top of the penis as explained above and you squeeze it firmly for about six seconds. This will have the immediate effect of curbing the man's urge to ejaculate and he will also lose some of his erection.

Pause for a while and then start stimulating him once more to bring back his erection.

While she is concentrating on pleasuring you, the man, you must concentrate on the sensations you feel inside your body, beyond the root of your penis. These are the sensations which tell you that you are about to come. Grow very conscious of them and once more, as you feel yourself on the point of coming, tell her so that she can rapidly apply the squeeze technique.

Do this four or five times during a session, so that the woman gradually increases her skill at squeezing. Many women hesitate to squeeze hard enough for fear of hurting the man, but do not forget that the penis, although sensitive, is able to withstand a fair amount of firm handling, unlike the clitoris which is a mass of nerve ends making it unable to tolerate too much direct pressure.

At first the man may ejaculate by mistake because the couple have got their timing wrong. For instance, he may wait too long before telling her to squeeze or she may hesitate before applying the pressure or squeeze too gently, for the reasons we described above. Neither should feel cast down by these temporary setbacks but do talk it over so that you both understand what went wrong. This way you will both learn more about each other. She is learning in a very intimate way exactly how his body responds to her attentions and he, by concentrating exclusively on his sensations, is learning to be very conscious of how his body builds up to climax.

These sessions should be repeated several times, preferably for at least a week, and day after day, with at least five experiences of squeezing in each session because, like any other skill, practice makes perfect. The couple cannot progress to the next stage until they are certain that they are both in control of his ejaculation. She will know how to apply the squeeze effectively on his signal, and he will find that he is able to hold out longer before asking her to squeeze and all the time he will be growing much more confident of his capacity to control ejaculation.

A couple who have been having regular intercourse up to now, even if it has not been satisfactory because of this problem of premature ejaculation, may find it hard to accept that during this first stage of therapy they must not have full intercourse. They can however, if they both agree, end the session by her stimulating him to ejaculation. As she is in charge of the therapy, he must ask her and, if she agrees, he must let her do the stimulation and not take over and masturbate himself.

Occasionally a man finds his tendency to ejaculate is increased by the squeeze technique. If you find this is happening to you, it is most probable that your partner is applying the squeeze too late because you, the man, are not conscious enough of the sensations inside your body leading up to ejaculation. Try to counteract this by instructing your partner to stimulate your penis more gently while you concentrate even more on discriminating these fine sensations so that you are ready to tell her to apply the squeeze sooner rather than later. However, if this difficulty persists, you will require personal advice from a sex therapist.

When you both feel that you have gained control of his ejaculation you can move on to the second stage where the same controlling technique is applied during penetration.

Start by mutually pleasuring and arousing each other so that he gets an erection and her vagina starts to swell and lubricate. Then the man lies on his back and the woman straddles him in a kneeling position.

When you both feel ready and his erection is strong enough, you, the woman, take his penis and guide it into your vagina, lowering yourself down the length of it. Both remain quiet and still. Enjoy the sensations.

She will be delighting in the sensation of a strong, hard, motionless penis filling her vagina. He will be focusing on feeling her soft, silky vagina into which his penis has slid like a finger into a glove. For both of you this may be quite a new experience if all you have ever known before is hasty penetration followed by even hastier ejaculation. Savour the experience and enjoy it.

At the beginning of this second stage of therapy you, the man, will probably feel unbearably excited and want to ejaculate almost as soon as you enter her vagina. Immediately you feel these sensations welling up, which by now you have learned to recognize and anticipate, you must indicate as much to your partner who remains in charge of the therapy. She will immediately raise herself off you, back to a kneeling position, and reach between her legs to grasp your penis and apply the squeeze.

Both of you know what to expect. Your erection will dwindle but she may remain aroused and gradually she can stimulate you to another erection and repeat the process. Sometimes she may enjoy manoeuvring the half limp penis into her vagina, allowing it to grow back to a full erection inside her.

Each time you do this, perhaps three or four times during a single session, you will find yourselves enjoying more and more the sensation of being interlocked without having to stimulate each other any further. The whole purpose of this 'quiet vagina' stage is to enable the man to learn to hold his erection inside her without ejaculating, and for her to experience the pleasure of being filled without the anxiety of it all coming to an end too soon.

Sometimes a couple find that the lack of stimulation causes the erection to disappear, in which case they must exercise just enough movement with each other to heighten their sexual excitement and so restore his erection and renew her lubrication.

You are ready for the third stage, probably in the third week, when you feel quite confident about the quiet vagina. The purpose of this final part of the therapy is to increase the amount of stimulation to the erect penis while still enabling the man to control ejaculation, so that he only comes when the woman too is ready and longing for orgasm: complete and satisfactory intercourse in fact.

The preliminaries are the same as for the quiet vagina stage but now, when it feels quite safe to hold the penis still inside the vagina, you can both start gently moving. She will rotate her vagina round your penis or move forwards and backwards or up and down. You will begin to thrust upwards, but always remembering to concentrate on your sensations and if you feel that you are about to climax but she is not yet ready for you, tell her so that she can immediately lift herself off you and apply the squeeze technique.

Neither of you will much enjoy doing this if you are both approaching an intense pitch of arousal; on the other hand, if you are coming too soon and she is not yet ready for you, the eventual feeling of let-down will be even worse. It is, therefore, important not to be tempted to be a little more easy-going at this late stage of the therapy because you both think that you have got the situation under control and that an occasional lapse will not matter.

Mistakes are one thing. They can happen to anybody and we can usually learn from them, especially when we understand how we made them. But carelessness is another. A couple who have got as far as the third stage have made enormous progress and if they can just hold on a little longer – literally – by continuing with the controlling techniques that they have been applying up to now, premature ejaculation will soon become a nightmare of the past. So, if he finds that the excitement of feeling her vagina moving round his penis is becoming too intense for him to be able to control his ejaculation, then he must tell her so that she can react appropriately. Applying the squeeze technique at this stage may interfere with mounting excitement, but by now they will both know enough about each other to re-establish arousal in the way that is right for them. •

Good sex is not about the rush to climax. It is about cooperating together for the climaxes that you both enjoy. Gradually you will find that it becomes less necessary for her to apply the squeeze technique during intercourse and he will find that he no longer worries about control. The squeeze technique is now part of your skill in love-making and you can use it in the future whenever you want it.

14. He never comes

The man who suffers from retarded ejaculation is like the woman who does not get an orgasm: he produces all the signs of arousal, including getting an erection and wanting a climax, but the trigger mechanism for producing ejaculation, although set, for some reason or another – nearly always psychological – just does not go off. Masters and Johnson call this disorder 'ejaculatory incompetence' and although it is essentially a problem connected with climax, the afflicted man sometimes develops impotence because of worrying so much about his failure to come. Some men are so anxious that their partner should not discover what is happening to them, or rather not happening, that they go to the lengths of pretending that they have indeed had an orgasm by thrusting until they hope that their partner is satisfied and then saying that they have had a climax themselves. This is exactly what so many women do, but the pretence, whether it comes from a man or a woman, is likely to have similar disastrous effects on a long-term relationship.

The problem is, however, one which affects relatively few men compared with the opposite male problem of premature ejaculation. One fairly foolproof way of knowing whether the problem is physical or psychological is to ask yourself – if this is your problem – whether you have wet dreams. If you do, then it is almost certain that the bodily mechanism is unimpaired but that there is a psychological concern which is putting the brakes on orgasm.

Occasionally a man will find that his erection fails with one woman but not with others. An example of this selective difficulty is illustrated by the problem of the man who had had reasonably satisfactory sexual relations with his wife until she had his children; from then on he found it quite impossible to climax inside her vagina because he said he looked on her as a mother and, therefore, someone untouchable; in other words, his unconscious reasoning processes had turned her into *his* mother as well as actually being the mother of his children. These situations are always complex. Further inquiry revealed that he was sexually active with large numbers of other women and had indeed been widely unfaithful to his wife for many years, nor did he experience this problem with any other woman. Undoubtedly, the marital relationship was deeply disturbed, although outwardly they presented a united and happy front. Inwardly he was racked by feelings of guilt towards the wife he no longer found sexually desirable but genuinely loved. He knew what effect the revelation of his infidelities would have on her, so he dared not discuss the situation with her nor suggest that they seek advice.

Conflicts of this nature which illustrate very ambivalent feelings towards a sexual partner are a typical cause of retarded ejaculation, itself a misnomer because frequently the ejaculation is so delayed that in reality it has become a non-event. Other typical conflict situations are those where a man feels deep concern about releasing his sperm, perhaps because he has been made to feel guilty about masturbation in youth and he brings this guilt to intercourse, or he may be worried about his bodily secretions and fear that his partner will be repelled by them. He may even be worried about impregnating her as we saw in Case History 10.

In milder cases, a small amount of alcohol or indulging in a favourite erotic fantasy – anything to get the mood exactly right – may release the catch. Sometimes talking about your fears and finding that your partner does not laugh at you may help, but usually the effort to relax in itself becomes so grim and intense that both man and woman end up feeling deeply frustrated and resentful. There is a popular belief that the woman who has such a sexual partner is really rather fortunate because his delay enables her to catch up with him and enjoy her orgasm at the same time. Since, however, his problem is that he cannot get a climax in intercourse, this is a myth and one which the woman involved finds bitterly ironic. Furthermore, she often feels rejected by his obvious inability to have pleasure with her and begins to wonder what is wrong with her. Unless they are able to face up to the situation and talk about it openly in the early stages, they may find themselves locked into a progressively deteriorating relationship. This is, of course, true for any sexual problem but in this particular case it is even more probable, because the nature of the disorder may also have something to do with the man's reserved and taciturn temperament.

The man who suffers from retarded ejaculation for whatever reason always has the same basic physical problem: he is unable to command his internal sphincter muscles. It is not a question of lack of control, as in premature ejaculation where a minimum degree of stimulation immediately prompts a man to open these muscles, thus setting off too early the trigger mechanism for ejaculation. Quite the reverse is true for the retarded ejaculator who is over-controlling, just as if he could not empty his bladder on demand. Try as he may, and we have seen anyway that trying is the worst thing he can do, he simply cannot relax and let his reflexes work naturally. Therefore, the purpose of the treatment designed for this type of sufferer is, first to teach him to relax and then gradually to take him through stages of approach to his partner until he feels able to ejaculate in her presence and, finally, within her.

As for premature ejaculation, it is essential that the man hands over control to his partner so that he may be left free to concentrate purely on his own pleasure and sensations. However, in all other respects, the treatment for retarded ejaculation is exactly the opposite. Whereas, in dealing with premature ejaculation, we talked about a gradual development of the capacity to accept more and more stimulation without ejaculating, starting with the 'quiet vagina', in the case of retarded ejaculation it is necessary for both man and woman to maximize the sensations which are flooding in.

Sexpiece 24

You will have already worked through to Sexpiece 14. Now create the circumstances of Sexpiece 15 and develop them in such a way that you are both giving amorous attention to every demand each is making of the other: stroking, massaging and committing yourselves totally to active pleasuring.

Let it centre more and more on genital stimulation, especially of the full shaft of the penis. Develop this any way you like, orally or manually. The purpose of this stage is for the woman to convey by everything she knows and looks and does and feels, how much she wants her lover's climax and to stimulate him accordingly. She will caress him and kiss him and use her body in every way she can think of to show him how much she enjoys being involved with him and his body. His penis will be the special focus of her attention and she will stimulate it on all the most sensitive parts in the ways he particularly likes.

The sexpieces will have taught you everything you need to know about asking for and giving pleasure. Remember, too, that language can be very arousing. Confide your fantasies. Both of you become completely involved in the rhythmic, rapid demands for masturbation. Plenty of body lotion is essential. Hold each other's hands round his penis. Agree together in your action that you are forcing a climax for your mutual fun. Let go.

This is the real breakthrough.

The next stage involves getting the man to ejaculate as close as possible to the entrance of the vagina. Again she will stimulate him and as soon as he feels aroused to the point of climax, he will signal her so that she can bring his penis to touch her vagina.

Once he has experienced ejaculating at the entrance to her vagina he will find that this has a tremendously releasing effect on his psyche. Seeing the pleasure which she gets from feeling his ejaculate spurt against her will reassure and encourage him, especially if his problem has been connected with a fear that his emissions are in some way repellent to his lover.

All that remains now for you both is to develop active, intense stimulation both outside and inside the vagina. One way of ensuring that he ejaculates inside the vagina is for her to lie back and hold his penis as he thrusts within her, meanwhile stroking or rubbing it. This is extra masturbatory stimulation. Incidentally, it is also a good way of stimulating a man who is suffering from partial impotence, the case where a man loses his erection just as he enters the vagina. •

Basically, retarded ejaculation is the physical expression of mental inhibition so, although we have suggested a stage-by-stage treatment, each couple should introduce their own extras for dealing with the man's particular inhibition. For example, the man who feels guilty about masturbating, either for himself or because he fears his lover's reaction, may be immensely reassured by watching her masturbate herself. Much unselfishness is required from the woman in this sexpiece, but watching her enjoy herself will help him to relax his control over himself and as he finds that his tension decreases, his physical sensitivity will increase.

15. She doesn't want me

It is not uncommon for a woman to be so frightened of being touched in her genital area and, particularly, of being penetrated, that any attempt to insert a finger or a penis into the vagina produces an automatic and reflex cramping of the muscles around the entrance to the vagina. The vagina closes up in a tight spasm like a fist being clenched and penetration becomes quite impossible. Women who suffer from this fear may not themselves understand why they react in this way to sexual advances and even the most tender and considerate of men will, quite naturally, begin to feel rejected and despairing if, time after time, he is unable to dissolve the incomprehensible defences put up by his lover. If he is not particularly confident of himself sexually he may react by suffering from occasional loss of erection.

Vaginismus, as this disorder is called, is the cause of many unconsummated marriages which sometimes continue for years before the couple finally decides to seek help. However, most women are as dismayed as their lovers by their extraordinary and uncontrollable reaction and will want to seek help as early as possible.

What causes the pathological fear of being touched? As with so many other sexual difficulties, it is often centred on a great deal of uncertainty or misunderstanding or real ignorance about sexual function. In this case, it is the vagina, and what happens to it when it is penetrated by a penis, which presents a frightening mystery to the uninstructed and inhibited woman who has been brought up to feel guilty and ashamed of her body. Like those women who resist letting themselves go in orgasm because they are frightened of what may happen to them, the woman who suffers from vaginismus may have dark fantasies about what will happen to her in intercourse. She may fear that the penis will destroy her in some way – rip her apart or damage other vital organs in her body. Many women who have never been able to allow intercourse are none the less torn apart by conflicting emotions. One part of them longs to be cured because they dread losing their lover, but the other part of them dreads cure because they fear the act of intercourse so deeply.

It can happen that a woman has suffered a traumatic sexual experience like rape or very clumsy early attempts at intercourse which were so painful and unpleasant that thereafter she reacts in a reflex way to any further approaches. She will be in a state of mental conflict, knowing with one part of her mind that her present lover does not want to hurt her and indeed would not hurt her, but another part of her mind recalls only the hateful memory and so her body reacts in self-protection. You know what happens if a piece of grit lodges in your eye. Your lid closes tightly and it needs considerable effort to hold it open in order to remove the grit. However, if you expect the grit to blow into your eye the lid flicks shut in anticipation. So it is with vaginismus and, plainly, it is very distressing both for the woman concerned and her lover. Ultimately it may destroy their relationship.

Fortunately, the cure is far less drastic and difficult than might be supposed. Whatever the underlying causes, vaginismus itself is a fear linked to a specific reflex and a fear of this type can never be overcome by the sufferer telling herself to try harder, because it is quite irrational. The woman is powerless to control her muscular reflexes which are responding to the messages sent out by the brain to counteract the fear, just as you are powerless to control your eyelid when grit strikes the eye. The cure concentrates on abolishing the fear by two means, both within the control of the woman herself.

If this is your problem, you must first of all instruct yourself about your body. Go back to Chapter 6, *Let's Look Again*, read it through carefully and discuss it with your lover. Until you know about your body and understand how it functions sexually, you will not be ready to start on the second part of the cure.

If you have not completed Sexpieces 1 to 8 and 10 to 14, then do them now, taking your time over several days. Should you not be able to complete numbers 12 and 13, especially 13, then you must seek the help of a therapist, but if you are now beginning to feel more at ease with your own body, then you are ready to do Sexpiece 25. The method we are about to describe depends first and foremost on you, enabling you to build up your own competence and confidence in yourself before you teach your lover.

Sexpiece 25

Make a time for yourself when you can be quiet, alone and undisturbed in your bedroom. Undress and lie down on your bed. Keep your eyes open and start exploring your vagina gently but deliberately. Do this by lying on your back with your legs slightly open and your hand resting on your pubic bone (where the hair is) letting your fingers curl downwards until you feel the outside lips (labia majora) which conceal the vaginal opening. Press your middle finger slightly into the slit between the lips so that it is lying along the outside of the vaginal opening. When you feel perfectly comfortable with your hand in that position, explore this inner area with the tip of your middle finger, possibly using some cream or KY jelly. You may feel your muscles tensing up; if so, try to relax them, but do no more with your finger than explore and satisfy yourself that you know exactly where your vaginal opening is. It is a good idea to use a mirror, placed between your legs or held with the other hand, so that you can see what you are doing.

When you have done this, you are ready to probe a little further on another occasion, but take this next stage as slowly as you want, so that you build up your confidence session by session. One reason why it is so much better for a woman to treat herself is because she knows better than anyone else possibly could how far to go and when to stop. However, it is important that at each session you should manage to enter your finger a little further.

You now know exactly where the vaginal opening is and you

will find a point where it feels tight and it is difficult to press any further. Your middle finger will probably have entered no further than half-way up to the first joint, but when you reach the point where your vagina feels tightly shut, let your finger rest there and then make a deliberate effort to tighten still further your vaginal muscles. Then relax them, just as if you were doing the exercise we described on page 61. Repeat this tightening and relaxing ten times at least. This exercise will make you more aware of these important vaginal muscles and enable you to bring them under your control.

At the next session start off in the same way, with your hand resting over your vaginal area and insert your finger until it reaches the point where it feels too tight to go any further. Again repeat the tightening and relaxing exercise, keeping your finger as far as it will go inside your vagina.

After you have done this several times, leave your muscles relaxed but your finger still inside and start using your muscles in a different way. Instead of tightening them, try pushing with them against the tip of your finger, exactly as if you were trying to pass water. At the same time, see if you can exert a little gentle pressure against them with your finger and, as you do so, you will feel your finger surrounded by muscles which begin to open up slightly in response to the downward pressure of your finger. If your vagina is not very moist, remember to use some cream. Increasing the finger pressure slightly will now let you explore the area of your vagina around which your muscles are contracting. When your finger feels surrounded by these muscles, again deliberately tighten them so that you can feel them gripping the end of your finger.

Once you have succeeded in inserting your finger to the point where you can easily tighten and relax your muscles round it, you have overcome the main hurdle. Now extend your confidence by improving on your skill.

First find out how far you can insert your finger. If you let it go in to its full length you will encounter a smooth knob at the end of your vagina which is called the cervix and which is where the neck of the womb meets the top of the vagina. The best way we know of describing the cervix is to compare it to the sensation you get by licking the tip of your finger and then rubbing it gently on the end of your nose. The cervix feels very much like the firm moist flesh that you feel by doing this.

Now try inserting two fingers. If you find yourself tensing up again as soon as something larger is introduced into your vagina, practise tightening and relaxing your vaginal muscles again. Once you are able to do this without feeling anxious, then you are ready to move on to the final stage of your treatment which involves your lover.

If he has previously tried to penetrate you without success he too may now be over-anxious about hurting you and very hesitant even about trying to insert his penis. Start by teaching him how to insert his fingers in the way you have taught yourself. (Smooth, short fingernails please!) Practise tightening and relaxing your muscles with his fingers inside.

The next stage is to be certain that your body is responding with sexual arousal, and Sexpiece 11 and the appropriate parts of Sexpiece 15 should be done. Do not rush at this stage. Make sure that you really have begun to feel aroused and are lubricating and that both of you are certain about the appearance of your genitals, knowing exactly where the opening of the vagina is, where the clitoris is and how your excitement is produced. As you are lubricating, your vagina will be increasing markedly in length and volume inside you and so preparing itself for the insertion of the erect penis which is considerably larger than two fingers. Now your reflexes are beginning to work for you instead of against you.

It is very important that the first attempts at intercourse should be done with you in the female superior position (see page 127). Before using the penis, practise kneeling in this position while inserting your fingers into your vagina so that you accustom yourself to sliding down on to something firm and upright.

When you feel aroused and receptive, encourage an erection in your lover and then lower yourself on to it from your kneeling position, straddling his body. The man must not thrust, but simply make his erection available for you to explore and enjoy. If you sense any return of the constriction, tighten and relax your vaginal muscles against the penis just as you did with your fingers. Learn to hold the shaft of the penis with your vaginal muscles. •

You are now ready to develop your sexual experience. Try Sex-pieces 16 and 17 together. You may find that the new experience of intercourse is so arousing for your lover that he ejaculates very quickly. If, after the first few times of intercourse you both feel that his climax is too swift, then have a look at Chapter 13 on controlling ejaculation (*He comes too soon*). You may need to learn the squeeze technique.

The treatment for curing vaginismus is relatively straight-forward, although it may take some weeks. It depends largely on the woman, but also requires patience and understanding from her partner. From her it requires a determination to solve her problem and a realistic appreciation that she may not particularly enjoy treating herself, especially at the beginning, because she is fighting to overcome a profound fear and this is never easy or pleasant. However, nothing we ask her to do involves pain or even minor discomfort and as she grows more comfortable with her body, she will find that her fears and tensions are dissolving. It will help immeasurably if she can confide in her lover and tell him how she is progressing.

16. Treat yourself to sex

You may have started to read this book with a mild feeling of curiosity about the title. We hope that now you have reached the last pages, you will understand its full significance – the enjoyment, delight and pleasure that two people can give to each other if they only know how. If you have found yourself identifying with any of the difficulties described, we hope, too, that our sexpieces have enabled you to treat yourself to a richer, happier sex life.

Just as the chapters are linked, so are the problems. However apparently one-sided it may at first appear, the couple who bring a problem to a sex therapist soon realize that even if it seems to start with one of them, it inevitably belongs to both of them in the end. Sexual problems have a ripple effect. One sets off another and, as they merge and swell and grow larger, they become more threatening to the whole relationship until, eventually, a couple may feel that there is no point any longer in trying to salvage what seems like hopeless wreckage. Better to cut loose and swim away before they go down with the remains. Often it is impossible for such a couple, who are caught up in the throes of their misery, to understand whether it is their incompatibility in other areas which has caused their sexual problems or whether it is the unsatisfactory nature of their sexual relationship which is poisoning other aspects of their life together. A couple who find that they are unable to share the intimacy of the sexpieces up to number 14 need more personal discovery through one-to-one counselling than they could hope to get from a book.

Fortunately, most sexual problems are basically simple in character and simple to solve, providing the couple concerned care enough for each other to want to discover what is going wrong and how to put it right. We have repeatedly stressed throughout this book how much we are affected by the society we live in, the aspirations we are brought up with, the expectations we have been encouraged to have of ourselves and of others, and the attitudes we have been taught to take about matters like sex and money and the 'right', that is to say, the correct or conventional way to behave towards others. Even those who seem more careless of the conventions may, in fact, be signalling an emotional rather than an intellectual reaction against their over-controlled and strict upbringing. We are, whether we like it or not, the creatures of our environment, and our sexual behaviour, to a large extent, reflects this dependency. This does not mean, however, that we must become victims. We *can* revise our views; we *can* change our behaviour.

While it is true that some people's sexual problems may be caused by physical factors or emotional events beyond their control, most people's difficulties arise out of negative attitudes which have been forced upon them from an early age and which they have never properly examined for themselves. Ignorance compounds this. They may have been told that sex was dirty or immoral or only acceptable when it was indulged in for the sake of producing children. They may not have been told very much about sex at all, picking up the little they do know in hints and whispers or from superficial articles. Even if ignorance is no longer your problem, and we hope it is not after reading this far, fear and guilt may still be a legacy which you cannot so easily shake off.

There is still a widespread bias against sex education among many people who broadly class themselves as educationalists, on the grounds that more or less anything is too much and that, given half a chance, all our children would be rushing off after school to try out what they had learnt in class for themselves. Many of them do just that, because they are intrigued by the mystery surrounding sex. Nobody has told them how powerful sexual feelings can be. Too often the experiment ends sadly, precisely because they have not been told enough, whereas it is fairly certain that those children who are sex-educated wisely and given all the facts will grow up reasonably well-adjusted sexual adults.

Unhappily there are not enough such people, because most of the schools and most parents simply do not do their job in this respect. Thus it is that fears, inhibitions and hang-ups are passed on from one generation to the next.

The main purpose of this book has been to offer you some ideas about getting in touch – with yourself, with your lover and with your feelings about yourself. We started by explaining what makes so many of us afraid of being intimate and why it is important to welcome intimacy and the joyous things that you can do with it. We then described in some detail how a couple can improve their total relationship by developing their physical understanding of each other. The remainder of the book has been devoted to describing specific therapy for specific problems. This is a book about sex, how to enjoy it as a treat and how to treat it. We make no apologies for concentrating exclusively on the sexual aspects of a relationship between two people because we believe that if this can be made more harmonious and satisfactory, other elements in the relationship will also benefit.

Good relationships grow out of feeling comfortable and at ease with one another because the people concerned feel good about themselves. Right at the very core of how we feel about ourselves is the feeling we have about our own bodies. If we like the way we look, the way we smell, the way our body responds to the messages our senses give us; if we enjoy using our bodies, anything from the most simple pleasure like walking over the fields on a wintry day or stretching ourselves in a hard game of tennis or swimming a few lengths, to the intense delight of losing ourselves in sex, then the pleasure that we take in our bodies and the confidence that we have in our ability to use our faculties to the full, will add immeasurably to the way we think about ourselves as a total person.

We have repeatedly stressed throughout this book how important it is to give ourselves time for sex, to make it a focal point of our life rather than something to be stumbled through in a mechanical dazed fashion at the end of a long, tiring day. Sex is a sensuous, stirring experience; it may be languorous and deliciously drawn out, a long, slow exploration of another body with our own

body or it may, on another occasion and in another mood, be rapid
and compulsive and drivingly passionate. All that it requires from
us to make good sex excellent is that we should willingly surrender ourselves to the eroticism that lingers in all of us, however
much we may have attempted to stifle it or ignore it. In an intimate relationship, forget what you have been told about self-control. Stop being afraid of exposing your vulnerability to someone
else. Ask yourself whether the voices of authority and disapproval
– your parents, former teachers, the neighbours – which come at
you in the middle of the night, matter. Are not the rules which
you have imposed on yourself to prevent yourself from becoming
'obsessed' with sex, self-inflicted?

Sex is a great pleasure of life, and one of the most valuable.
Nevertheless, there are times when we need it and want it more
than at others, and there are people we love and respect with
whom sex once seemed essential and no longer is, and others to
whom we feel equally drawn but with whom we have never
wanted to be involved sexually. Nobody should feel obliged to
have sex out of gratitude or respect or because it is expected, or
because everybody is having it or, saddest of all, out of sheer boredom. Ideally, sex is a deliberately chosen pleasure, but if two
people have a relationship together in which sex at least started
by being an essential element, then it seems a pity if it is allowed
to wither away for no better reason than lack of attention.

Relationships are like trees. Given the right conditions, they
shoot up and develop branches, grow leaves and fruit and become
strong, well-shaped and firmly rooted in the common soil of the
understanding and affection which unites two people. Given unfavourable conditions, like an early lack of love and security in a
child's upbringing, or instilled notions of fear and shame about
our bodily functions, the relationship may develop but, like a tree
leaning out from the side of a steep, windswept cliff, it may
become tenacious and stunted – two people clinging to each other,
not out of love or a warm pleasure in each other's company, but
because they are afraid of being cast off. If the early conditions are
very adverse, say for example that neither of them has ever truly
succeeded in establishing a positive and intimate relationship with

anyone, whether sexual or not and for whatever reasons buried in their past, then the tree may never take root at all.

We start learning about relationships in the very earliest emotional experiences of our life, in our relationships with our parents and family and, later, through the wider circle of friends and teachers. As young children we have very little control over what happens to us, whether good or bad. It is only as we move into adolescence and young adulthood that we begin to learn how to manage relationships for ourselves, and it is at this time that our sexuality plays an increasingly important role. If we have always been encouraged to be trusting, open and giving, then it is likely that we will be able to adapt with reasonable facility to whatever circumstances are presented to us in our personal relationships. If, however, we have not been so fortunate in our early upbringing, then it may be more difficult for us to cope with difficult situations, which may not always be of our own making.

Environment is not the only important formative element in our personality. Each one of us is a unique, unrepeatable mixture of genes, inherited from our mother and father, which are transformed into attributes like height, size and colouring, or being gifted with one's hands, or exceptionally athletic or very musical. Again we have no control over what is meted out to us, or the proportions, but we do have control over how we use them; and, as members of the human race, we do share common needs and characteristics. We need love, support and sympathy from the moment we are born and becoming an adult does not reduce our need. We stunt ourselves if we think it does. Children who are deprived of emotional sustenance will, if they survive childhood, become detached, unresponsive adults, incapable either of giving or of receiving love. Fortunately, human beings are essentially hardy and adaptable, and many people have lived through an incredibly rigorous and unhappy childhood to become mature, generous adults, for whom a fulfilled sexual relationship may be the first opportunity they have had to explore their emotional needs wholeheartedly.

This is a book about basics. We have not wanted to add to the already long list of manuals which tend to assume that their readers are all well-informed, well-adjusted and perfectly happy with themselves and their sexual partners – and the only reason for picking up yet another book on the subject of sex is their natural interest in the subject, and an idle curiosity to see whether they can pick up one or two new wrinkles. We are not writing for armchair sexologists or for advanced lovers, but for people who may, or may not, be highly experienced sexually and who, for reasons beyond their comprehension, find that sex is not the pleasure that they would like. They want to know why and they want to know what they can do about it. It is for people who are seeking honest answers together.

What we have not talked about in this book are the variations of sexual behaviour. Some people get fixed at a certain stage in their sexual development so that they then find that they can only express themselves in a sexually variant way such as in masochism or sadism or voyeurism or fetishism. Nor have we talked about homosexuality in any specific fashion, although a great deal of what we have said about treating yourself to sex applies equally to anyone in a homosexual relationship. Other deliberate omissions include any discussion of sex in later life, whether about the difficulties or the adaptations that people may have to make. But everything that we have written about seeking and giving pleasure, understanding oneself and learning how to meet one's own sexual needs as well as another's on a mutually satisfactory basis, is relevant to sexual function at all ages. Indeed, a couple may well find that it is when their family has grown up and left home and the struggles and preoccupations of the first twenty-odd years are behind them, that the time is ripe for a profound re-evaluation of their whole relationship, including its sexual aspects. If they continue to care for one another, they may reap long-term dividends by making a real investment in renewing the quality of their sex life.

We are well aware that this book has in the main been directed towards couples, but the essential message and information it contains are as relevant to the single person's life as to those who are currently in a stable and long-established relationship. How to feel good about one's own body, how to enjoy it and, above all, how to take time to delight in it and banish any inappropriate feelings of guilt is knowledge that is just as available and necessary to the single person. We each of us carry the responsibility for enjoying our own bodies. When we can do that, we have something and everything to share.

References and resources

1. WILLIAM MASTERS and VIRGINIA JOHNSON: *Human Sexual Response* (Little, Brown & Co., 1966); *Human Sexual Inadequacy* (Little, Brown & Co., 1970). These two volumes describe the research and clinical work of Masters and Johnson. For useful summaries containing the main findings see the following paperbacks: RUTH BRECHER and EDWARD BRECHER: *An Analysis of Human Sexual Response* (Panther, 1968); FRED BELLIVEAU and LIN RICHTER: *Understanding Human Sexual Inadequacy* (Hodder, 1971).
2. ERIC BERNE: *Sex in Human Loving* (Pelican, 1973).
3. DESMOND MORRIS: *Intimate Behaviour* (Corgi, 1973).
4. SHERE HITE: *The Hite Report* (Tamlyn Franklin, 1977).
5. HELEN SINGER KAPLAN: *The New Sex Therapy* (Penguin, 1978).
6. BETTY DODSON: *Liberating Masturbation* (Bodysex Designs, New York, 1974).
7. WENDY COOPER: *No Change* (Hutchinson, 1975).
   (For information about menopause clinics see also *The Women's Directory* by FAULDER, JACKSON and LEWIS, Virago, 1976.)
8. Boston Women's Health Collective: *Our Bodies Ourselves* (Simon & Schuster, 1976).
9. Sexual function aids can be ordered by post from Phyllis Wright (Health & Hygiene) Ltd, 34 St George's Walk, Croydon, Surrey, CRO 1YJ, tel: 01-681 1298. A catalogue will be sent on request.
10. Nancy Friday: *My Secret Garden* (Virago, 1975).

Bookshop

All the books referred to above can be ordered for delivery by post through the bookshop of The National Marriage Guidance Council, Little Church Street, Rugby, tel: Rugby 73241.

Clinics

The National Marriage Guidance Council is also setting up clinics for the specific treatment of sexual difficulties as well as maintaining their long-established counselling services for help with a wide variety of marital and relationship difficulties. The address of your nearest branch will be in the telephone book.

The Association of Sexual and Marital Therapists has compiled a list of all the centres where direct treatment for sexual difficulties is available. For a complete up-to-date list, including names of individual therapists you or your doctor can contact, send a large stamped addressed envelope to the Association at 79 Harley Street, London W1.

Index

More about Penguins and Pelicans

For further information about books available from Penguins please write to Dept EP, Penguin Books Ltd, Harmondsworth, Middlesex UB7 0DA.

In the U.S.A.: For a complete list of books available from Penguins in the United States write to Dept CS, Penguin Books, 625 Madison Avenue, New York, New York 10022.

In Canada: For a complete list of books available from Penguins in Canada write to Penguin Books Canada Ltd, 2801 John Street, Markham, Ontario L3R 1B4.

In Australia: For a complete list of books available from Penguins in Australia write to the Marketing Department, Penguin Books Australia Ltd, P.O. Box 257, Ringwood, Victoria 3134.

In New Zealand: For a complete list of books available from Penguins in New Zealand write to the Marketing Department, Penguin Books (NZ) Ltd, P.O. Box 4019, Auckland 10.

Sex Guides for the Young

BOY GIRL MAN WOMAN
B. H. Claësson

Here at last is a book devoted to the special needs of the young. Informative and sympathetic, it enables them to increase their sexual awareness and enjoy their own sexuality.

'*Boy Girl Man Woman* is excellent. It provides clarity and humanity in just the right mixture. Adolescents will find it immensely helpful and reassuring' – James Hemming

BOYS AND SEX
Wardell B. Pomeroy

Dealing in a clear and honest manner with all aspects of sexual development, from masturbation and homosexuality to petting and intercourse, and with an enlightening 'question and answer' section, this book will guide boys towards a guilt-free understanding of the emotions and reactions which they will experience throughout adolescence.

GIRLS AND SEX
Wardell B. Pomeroy

After describing the female organs and their functions, he introduces the young reader to the kind of physical changes and urges she must normally encounter in her sex life. Dr Pomeroy's subsequent handling of menstruation, petting, intercourse, pregnancy, venereal disease, masturbation and homosexuality are designed to allay anxiety and usher a young girl 'into the adult world with the best prospects for happiness'.

THE NEW SEX THERAPY
Helen Singer Kaplan

One of the most important advances since the Victorian era
has been the recent recognition that sexual problems both
exist and can be solved, within or without marriage.

The more common difficulties experienced – 'impotency' in
men, 'frigidity' in women, or what are euphemistically called
'bed hang-ups' – are sympathetically dealt with in Helen
Singer Kaplan's valuable and professional study. She places
treatment of sexual dysfunction, for the first time, on a solid,
scientific basis and, equally important, manages to convey
how the breakdowns commonly inherent in a sexual
relationship can be effectively treated and solved.

SEXUAL DEVIATION
Anthony Storr

This book is a brief account of the common types of sexual
behaviour which are generally considered perverse or deviant,
together with explanations of their origins.

Anthony Storr shows how sexual deviations can result from
inner feelings of sexual guilt and inferiority which have
persisted from childhood. It may seem a far cry from the
lover's pinch to the whip of the sado-masochist, but embryonic
forms of even the most bizarre deviations can be shown to
exist in all of us . . .

OUR BODIES OURSELVES
A *health book by and for women*
Boston Women's Health Book Collective
British edition by Angela Phillips and Jill Rakusen

Our Bodies Ourselves was written by and for women in
response to a need for all of us to learn about our bodies in
order to have control over our lives. The book seeks to
communicate our excitement about the power of shared
information; to assert that we are the best experts on
ourselves and our feelings; to continue the collective struggle
for adequate health care.

The material covered includes anatomy, sexuality,
relationships, lesbianism, nutrition and health, venereal
disease and common ailments, birth control, abortion,
considering parenthood, childbearing, menopause, the health
care system and how to use it.

'Every woman in the country should be issued with a copy
free of charge' – *Mother & Baby*

FROM WOMAN TO WOMAN
Lucienne Lanson

Completely up-to-date, detailed, and authoritative, this book
encompasses not only such common areas of concern as the
gynaecological examination, irregular periods, menstrual
cramps, fertility, and problems of the menopause – all
considered from a psychological as well as a physical point of
view in easy-to-follow question-and-answer form – but far
more.

THE BODY
Anthony Smith

Anthony Smith examines, with rare individuality, the human body, its functions, its abilities and its peculiarities. Sex and reproduction, being the mainstay of the life-cycle, form his central theme; this is supplemented by an unexpected variety of information about such things as inheritance, circumcision, haemophilia, twinning, and many other topics seldom explored or explained.

Later chapters deal with other bodily functions, such as the senses, digestion, sleep, and the skeleton, all accompanied by relevant, curious facts, which make the subject all the more fascinating.

THE MASSAGE BOOK
George Downing

With this simple manual you can practise and perfect the art of massage.

The instructions, which are clearly illustrated and easy to follow, detail the strokes and positions to be adopted for massaging every part of the body from the top of the head to the tips of the toes.

Massage is an act of healing and a powerful means of communicating without words. In order to convey the full range and effect of the art, the author outlines its wider 'philosophy' and its links with oriental cults. He includes, too, chapters on meditation and on massage for lovers.